READER'S DIGEST BASIC GUIDE

The maintenance of BICYCLES

CONTENTS

Owning a bicycle 2

Basic types of bicycle 4

Parts of a bicycle 6

Inspection and maintenance 8

Tool kits and lubrication 8-9

Chains 10

Valves 11

Wheels 12

Gears 16

Brakes 22

Movable parts ... 28

Handlebars 29

Frames 30

Pedals 34

Mudguards 35

Crankset 36

Lights 38

MOST OF THE TEXT AND ILLUSTRATIONS IN THIS BOOK ARE TAKEN FROM 'READER'S DIGEST REPAIR MANUAL'
ADDITIONAL ILLUSTRATIONS FOR THIS EDITION BY:
NORMAN LACEY AND **HAYWARD AND MARTIN**

TECHNICAL ADVISER: DOUGLAS DODSWORTH

THE PUBLISHERS WOULD LIKE TO THANK
FREEWHEEL, 275 WEST END LANE, LONDON NW6 1QS
AND **MEND-A-BIKE,** 15 PARK WALK, LONDON SW10 0AJ,
FOR THEIR HELP AND CO-OPERATION.

PUBLISHED BY THE READER'S DIGEST ASSOCIATION LIMITED
LONDON NEW YORK CAPE TOWN MONTREAL SYDNEY

Owning a bicycle

A bicycle owner's responsibility

A bicycle rider is responsible for maintaining his machine in good order, so that there is no danger of mechanical failure affecting his own or other people's safety. He should also make sure that his bicycle is suited to his size.

Bicycles bought through mail order should be carefully assembled for road use according to the maker's instructions, and all nuts, bolts and screws securely tightened. If you experience any difficulty, have the job done at a repair shop.

Fitting the bicycle to the rider

For safe and comfortable riding, a bicycle must fit its intended rider. Make sure of this when choosing a machine. Bicycles for adults are made in frame sizes varying from 18 in. (460 mm) to 25 in. (630 mm)—the length of the seat mast tube from saddle to pedals.

When standing astride the bicycle, you should have at least 1 in. (25 mm) clearance above the horizontal crossbar—or an imaginary crossbar on a woman's bicycle or a folding bicycle. You should also be able to touch the ground with the soles and heels of your feet.

Adjust the saddle (see p. 28) so that the seated rider, with his knee slightly bent, can place the ball of his foot on the pedal when at its lowest position.

When buying a bicycle you should ask the dealer to let you have a trial ride. That way you can make sure that the machine is the right one for you. After two or three weeks' use, a new bicycle will probably need some adjustment. Make sure that your dealer agrees to do this for you free of charge.

Adjust the handlebars (see p. 28) so that the seated rider can reach them comfortably and can operate the brakes and any gear controls without difficulty. The most comfortable position, other than for sports or racing machines, is generally with the top of the handlebars about level with the saddle.

There are two ways of testing the quality of the frame. Firstly, raise the cycle some 2 in. (50 mm) from the ground and then drop it. The better the frame, the more the cycle will reverberate and bounce. Secondly, stand to the side of the cycle and hold the handlebars with one hand and the saddle with the other. Tilt the cycle away from you and place one foot on the bottom bracket axle and push gently. The better the frame, the more it will flex and spring back at you when you release your foot.

When choosing a child's bicycle, make sure the rider can place both feet flat on the floor while astride the saddle. For very young learners, stabiliser wheels to keep the bicycle upright help to give confidence at first.

Safety helmets

Most serious injuries and deaths involving cyclists are caused by blows to the head—such as falling and striking the head against the kerb. Safety helmets give protection against impact and penetration in the event of a road accident. The outer shell is made of extremely strong and durable plastic, and a polyester lining absorbs shock. The helmets are ventilated to minimise the build-up of heat—a potential source of discomfort. They have a fully adjustable nylon strap and a locking device that prevent them from slipping.

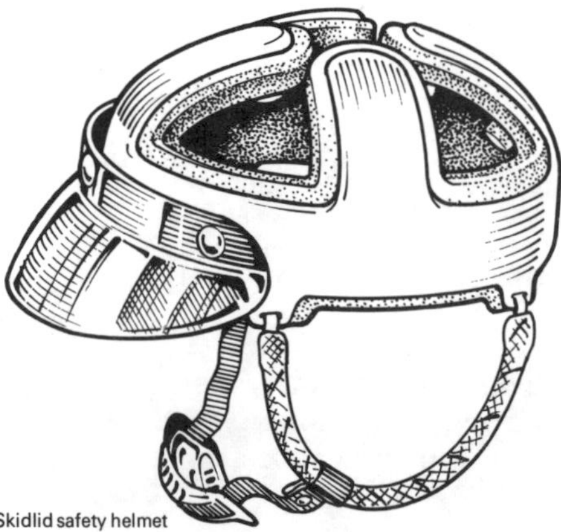

Skidlid safety helmet

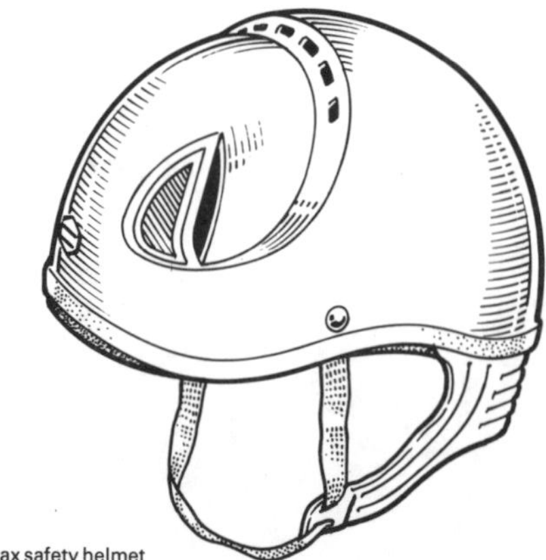

Max safety helmet

Guarding against theft

All bicycles have a maker's frame number stamped beneath the bottom bracket, on the seat lug or on the left side of the rear wheel. You should keep a record of the number so that your bicycle can be identified in the event of theft.

To help the police to quickly trace the owner of a recovered stolen bicycle, some dealers will stamp bicycles on purchase with a code combining the post code and house number of the owner. A 'Coded Cycle' sticker on the frame may help to deter thieves. Upon change of ownership, the code can be cancelled and replaced.

There are various kinds of padlocks, chains and U-shaped, metal locking devices—such as Kryptonite and Citadel—on sale. Case-hardened, U-shaped locks give far greater protection than wire rope locks—which thieves can cut through in a matter of seconds. The U-shaped locks are expensive, but the outlay is justified by the protection provided.

If the U-shaped locks are too expensive for your pocket, buy a 3 ft length of heavy duty, case-hardened chain and a padlock with a case-hardened coupling link. Such an item should cost about a third of the price of a Kryptonite or Citadel.

Whatever type of lock you settle for, always make sure to attach it—and the cycle—to a fixed object such as an iron railing or lamp-post. Fit the lock through the front wheel *and* the cycle frame—otherwise a thief will be able to steal the machine, minus the front wheel.

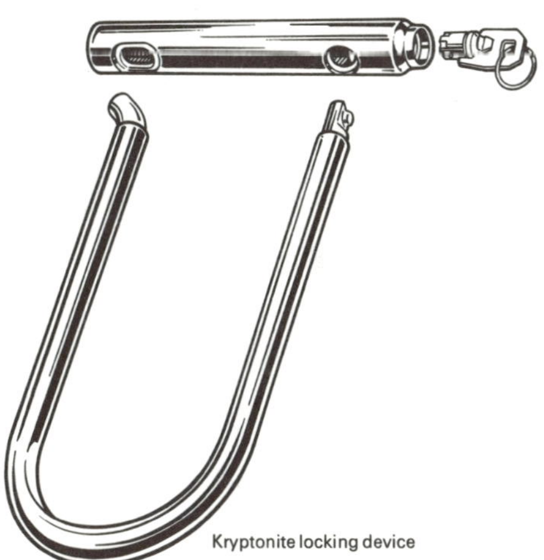

Kryptonite locking device

SAFE CYCLING

DO'S

DO check that the brakes are working properly before riding your bicycle. Make sure that the tyres are firmly inflated and that the wheel nuts are screwed tight.

DO make sure that the bell or warning device is working, and use it to give warning of your approach.

DO glance behind to make sure the way is clear before moving off or turning.

DO use arm signals clearly and in good time to show that you intend to turn to the left or the right.

DO keep both hands firmly on the handlebars except when signalling.

DO comply with all road signs, such as traffic lights, halt signs, one-way streets and pedestrian crossings.

DO keep to the left and ride in a straight line. Never swerve from side to side or weave in and out of traffic.

DO watch out for cars pulling out into traffic. Give clearance to parked cars, whose doors may be opened outwards in front of you without warning.

DO keep a look-out for animals or children who might suddenly run into the road.

DO make sure that your lights are working before riding at night, and that the rear and spoke reflectors are efficient. It is a good idea to wear light-coloured or reflecting clothing. Reflective belts, arm bands, ankle bands and sleeveless jackets are available.

DO ride slower than usually in wet weather and apply your brakes sooner than in dry conditions. No brakes work as well in wet weather as they do in the dry.

DO try to keep at least a bicycle length away from a vehicle that is in front of you.

DO wear bicycle clips, or tuck your trouser ends into your socks, to prevent the clothing from catching on a part of the machine.

DO concentrate on the task of cycling at all times. Never let yourself be distracted — by listening-in on a radio headset, for example.

DON'TS

DON'T carry other riders, except children on a properly fitted rear seat.

DON'T carry packages or wear clothes that may impede control of the bicycle, that obstruct your vision, or that may catch on the machine.

DON'T ride on the footpath; it is a danger to pedestrians and against the law.

DON'T hang on to the back of vehicles in order to get a 'free ride,' and never race or try stunt-riding on a public road.

DON'T overtake vehicles on the outside of the road in the face of oncoming traffic.

Basic types of bicycle

Choosing a bicycle

Today, with more and more people taking to the road on two wheels, there are bicycles to fit every type of requirement—from full-sized adult bicycles to 'fun' bicycles for children. Before buying any type of machine you should consider exactly why you want it—for example, for commuting to work in a city or for speeding about the countryside at weekends. The following descriptions of eight types of bicycle should help you to make the right choice.

Tourist cycles
Touring machines generally weigh about 35 lb (16 kg) and are designed for practical everyday use. They have large wheels, three to five-speed gears and straight handlebars for more relaxed riding. They can be fitted with saddlebags or panniers.

Roadster cycles
Strong, heavy, large-wheeled bicycles weighing about 50 lb (23 kg), roadsters are built for hard use, including trade deliveries. They usually have rod brakes and three-speed gears.

Sports cycles
Designed for speed, balance and control, sports cycles are lightly built and often have alloy components to keep down weight, which is generally 25–30 lb (11–14 kg). They have dropped handlebars for streamlined riding and Derailleur gears for fast acceleration. The wheels are normally large and slim to reduce friction with the road surface. Sports cycles have either full-length or half-length mudguards of lightweight plastic or alloy.

Folding shopper cycles
With their small wheels and small frames, folding shoppers are adaptable and easy to manoeuvre. Both saddle and handlebars have lever-operated adjusters and there is no crossbar, so that they can be used by all members of the family. They are lightweight—18–25 lb (8–11 kg)—with plenty of room for carriers. A locking mechanism in the frame enables them to be folded in two for easy storage or packing into a car boot. They are not designed for long-distance cycling.

BMX-type cycles
Ruggedly built bicycles such as the BMX are intended for knock-about use rather than for speed or long-distance cycling. They are small-wheeled, small-framed machines with high handlebars that can be easily manoeuvred at low speeds, and are designed for children from nine to 16 years old. They generally weigh 30–35 lb (14–16 kg), and their wide, heavy, studded tyres give a good grip on road or dirt surfaces. Brakes are usually front calipers and rear hubs.

Children's cycles
Most cycles for young children have a caliper front brake, although some models are also fitted with a coaster brake. The wheels are small and thick and there is often a rear container for holding toys and so on. A pair of extra-small wheels can be fitted at the back so that the machines will not topple sideways.

Tandem cycles
Designed for two riders, tandems are most often touring machines and can weigh from about 40–90 lb (18–41 kg). Some have a crossbar at the front position but not at the rear, and are termed ladyback; those with a through crossbar are termed double gents. Some makes can be fitted with a sidecar for carrying children.

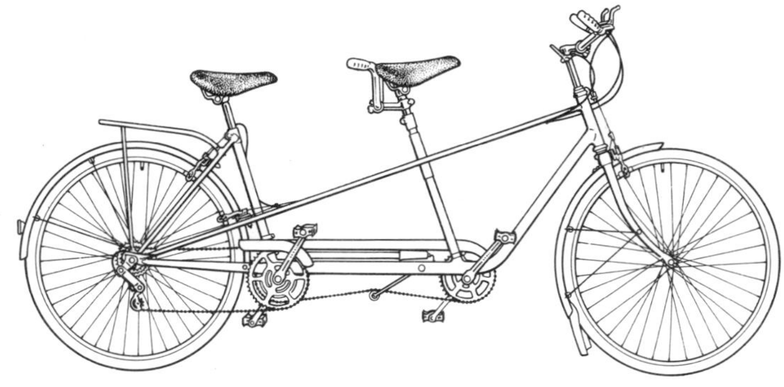

Adult tricycles
These strong, three-wheeled cycles have three-speed gears and hub brakes. They are ideal for shopping and for the cyclist who does not trust himself on a two-wheeled machine. However, tricycles have to be steered around corners—and care must be taken not to raise the outside rear wheel and so bring the cycle over on top of you. Particular care must be taken when negotiating a downhill bend, as the cycle is then even more inclined to overbalance. In place of the roomy, rear shopping basket, seats can be fitted for carrying children.

Parts of a bicycle

Getting to know your machine

Once you have chosen the right bicycle for your purpose, you should familiarise yourself with the various parts of the machine. There are six major parts of any bicycle—frame, wheels, tyres, brakes, gears and lights—and they come in the following forms and sizes.

Frames
Bicycle frames are usually made of tubular steel. Tubes may be seamed or seamless, and have walls that are of even thickness throughout or double-butted—thicker inside at the ends. The tube joints may be butted and welded, or be fitted into lugs and brazed (heated and sealed with brass or silver). The strongest and most expensive frames have seamless, double-butted, lug-jointed tubes. Frames which have no crossbar have two tubes leading from the head of the frame to the rear-fork ends.

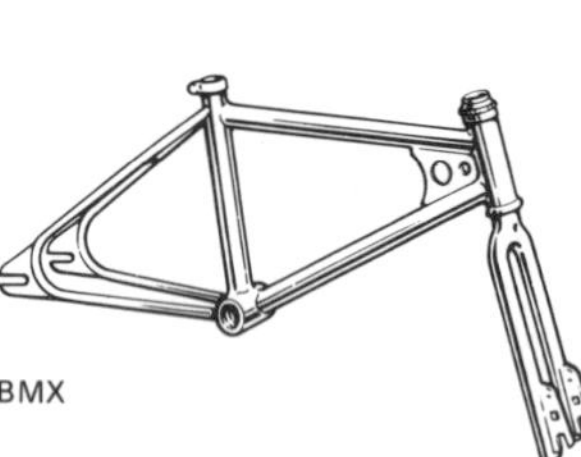

BMX

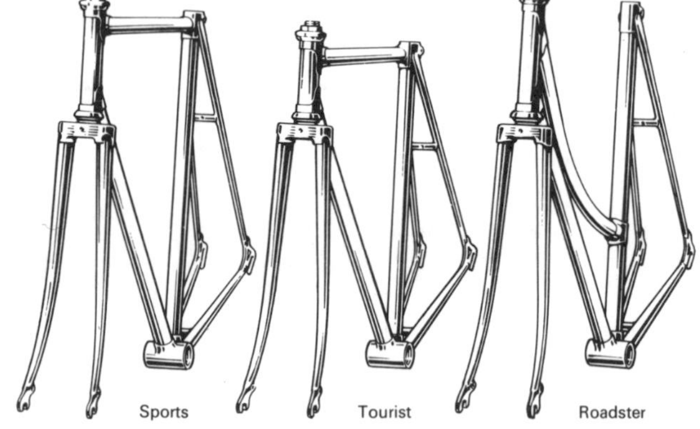

Sports Tourist Roadster

Wheels
Large wheels are usually about 26 in. (655 mm) in diameter, small wheels 16 or 20 in. (400 or 500 mm). Rim widths are generally $1\frac{1}{4}$ in. (sports) or $1\frac{3}{8}$ in., or $1\frac{1}{2}$ in. on a roadster; they may be $1\frac{3}{4}$ in. on a trade bicycle and $2\frac{1}{8}$ in. on a BMX-type bicycle. Rims are made of durable steel or lighter and more expensive aluminium alloy. Rim profiles vary in shape—the main types are Endrick (used with caliper brakes), Westwood (used with rod brakes), and Westrick (used with either). Small wheels allow for a lighter, more adaptable bicycle that is easy to manoeuvre; but large wheels give an easier ride. Sports and racing machines often have quick-release hubs; for quick wheel removal, they are secured by locking cams released by a lever instead of nuts that have to be undone with a spanner.

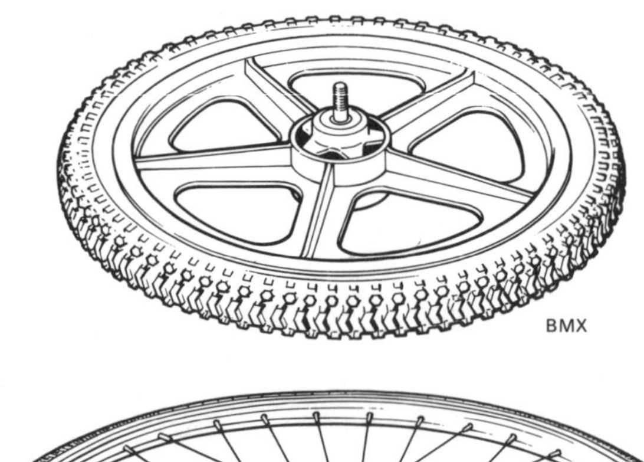

BMX

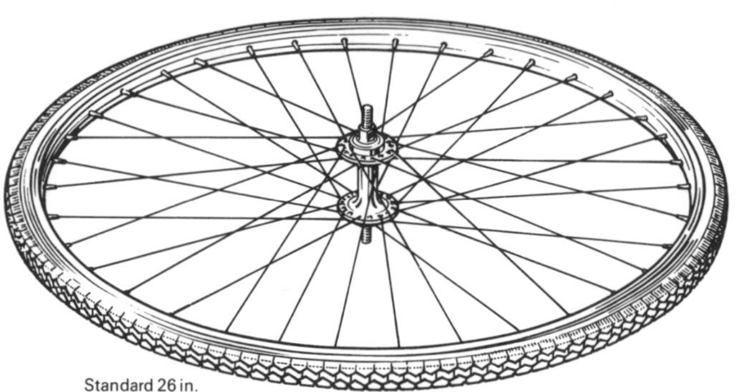

Standard 26 in.

Tyres
Most bicycle tyres are treaded rubber casings, with separate inflatable inner tubes. The maximum pressure for inflation is marked on the cover sidewall—for example, 85 psi (pounds per square inch) on a $27 \times 1\frac{1}{4}$ in. tyre. High-pressure tyres such as 85 psi are usually confined to sports machines. Coverings are now available for inserting between the tyre cover and inner tube to reduce the likelihood of a puncture. One-piece tubular tyres are used on racing bicycles. These tyres are very slim and lightweight and can be inflated to 120 psi. However, they puncture easily.

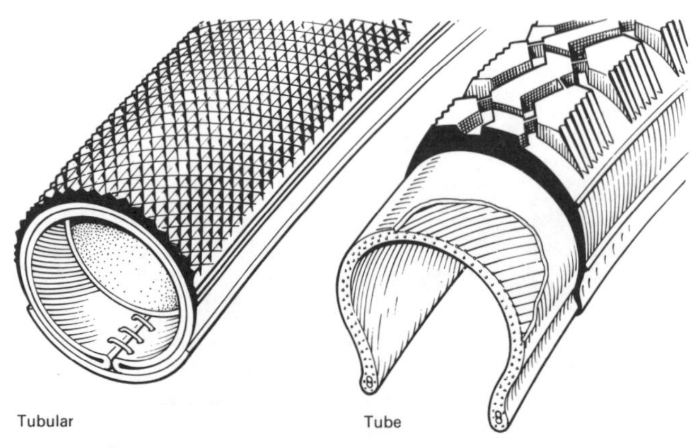

Tubular Tube

Parts of a bicycle

Brakes

Caliper-type, hub or coaster brakes are the three main kinds of bicycle brake. Calipers have blocks that grip the wheel rim and are operated by cables from a lever on the handlebars; the caliper may have a side-pull or centre-pull cable. A similar arrangement is the rod-pull or roller-lever brake, with stirrup-mounted brake blocks acting on the wheel rim. Brake blocks are normally made of rubber and are sometimes studded; their shapes vary, and must be related to the wheel rim profile. Leather blocks are now available for use with steel rims, and fibre blocks for steel or alloy rims; these are more effective than rubber in wet weather. Hub, or drum, brakes have expanding shoes encased in the wheel hubs and are operated by cable from a handlebar lever or twist-grip. Today they are found mainly on tandems or BMX-type bicycles, and replacement shoes are not easy to get. Coaster brakes are encased in the rear hub and operated by back-pedalling. They are found mostly on children's bicycles and on models made in Holland.

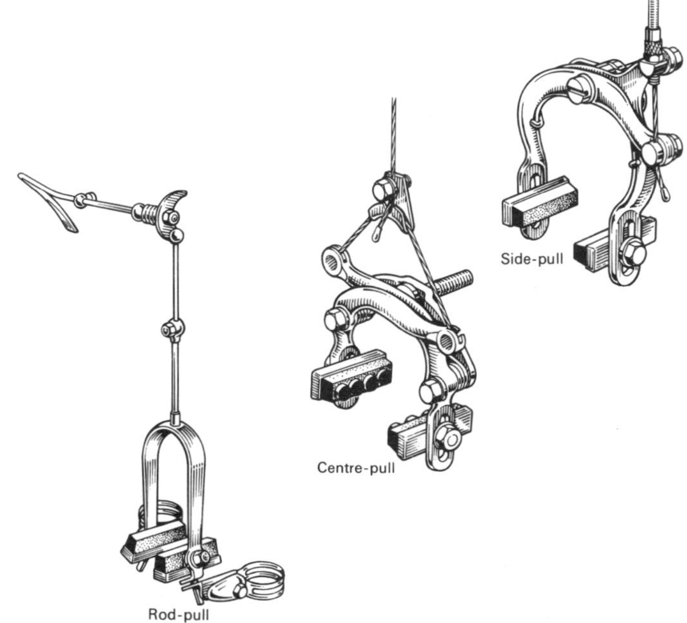

Gears

Sports and racing bicycles have Derailleur gears, a mechanism that shifts the driving chain to different-sized cog wheels according to the gear selected; 5, 10, 12 or 15 speeds may be available, operated by cables from a trigger or lever on the handlebars or down tube. Hub gears, encased in the rear hub, have 3–5 speeds and are operated by cable from a trigger, lever or handlebar twist-grip. They are not as efficient as Derailleur gears and make the bicycle heavier. However, they are convenient as they are protected from dirt and rain and so need less maintenance. Major overhauls are best done professionally as the work calls for skill and experience. Hub gears and coaster brakes are available in a combined unit. Machines with one gear are called single-speed.

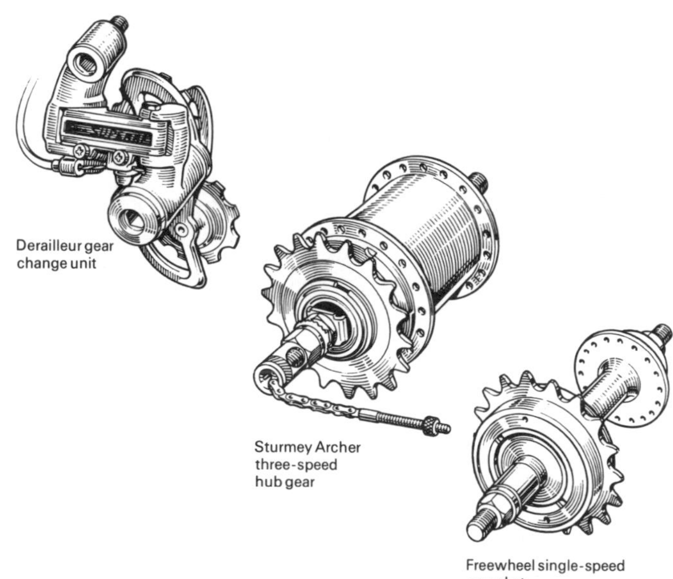

Lights

Battery lamps have the advantage of giving a constant, steady light. The heavier type are screwed on to a bracket and the lightweight, portable type slide on to a clip and can be removed—to defeat thieves—when the cycle is left unattended. A dynamo driven by the rear tyre provides bright front and rear lights at fast speeds; but these operate only when the bicycle is moving. Dynohub lighting has a generator built into the front wheel hub, and can be combined in a system with battery lamps. Lamps should not be fitted to a front fork unless there is a built-in holder. It is dangerous to fit a clamp-held lamp to the front fork as it can slip and catch in the wheel.

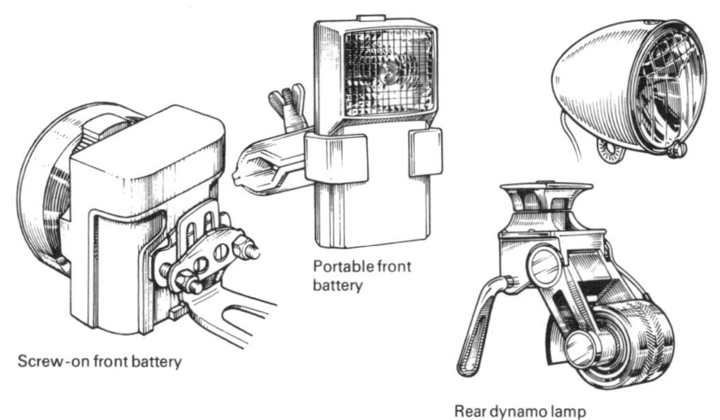

Inspection and maintenance

Tool kits

Maintenance

A well-cared-for bicycle should last its owner for a lifetime—and, barring accidents, not involve anyone in any expensive and time-consuming repairs. Make regular inspections—about once a fortnight if the bicycle is in daily or regular use—to ensure that all the nuts, bolts and screws are tightly fixed and that no parts are badly worn or in any way damaged. Oil the parts indicated below and check all the following parts, adjusting and replacing as necessary.

Tyres
Keep the tyres firmly inflated. The walls should feel hard, with no give, when pressed between the finger and thumb. If you use a calibrated pump, do not inflate beyond the maximum pressure on the tyre wall, for example 55 lb (25 kg). A soft tyre may indicate that you have a slow puncture or a faulty valve. Replace tyres which have badly worn or damaged treads. (See also p. 12. Mending a puncture. Fitting a new rim tape. Refitting a tyre and tube.)

Brakes
With caliper-type brakes, keep the brake blocks adjusted to the rim and replace worn or missing blocks (see p. 22). Make sure there is no grease or oil on the wheel rims, as this will cause blocks to slip and so reduce braking power. Brake cables stretch with use. Adjust them regularly and replace worn or damaged cables. Do not 'kink' the cable. Make sure that rod brakes move freely on pivot points and straighten any bent rods. (See pp. 22–27. Adjusting brakes and fitting new blocks. Centre-pull brake. Replacing and adjusting brake cables. Brake adjustment. Fitting new front shoes. Renewing the bearings.)

Coaster brakes
Check that the brakes operate smoothly without locking or grabbing. Rough or grating movement indicates that the bearings need renewing. Make sure the brake arm is securely fastened to the bicycle frame.

Gears and gear controls
Make sure Derailleur gears are properly adjusted. Do not shift gear lever except when pedalling, and never let the bicycle rest on the gear units. When changing gear on a three-speed hub, back-pedal slightly so the gear engages properly. Leave three-speed hub gears in third gear overnight so that the cable is not stretched. Put Derailleur gears in fifth gear overnight. (See pp. 17–21. Renewing a twist-grip control gear cable. Replacing a gear cable. Adjusting a five-speed gear. Removing a Derailleur-gear rear wheel. Adjusting a ten-speed gear. Replacing a sprocket. Removing and replacing a five-speed cog.)

Wheels
Make sure that the axle nuts are tight and that no spokes are loose, bent or missing. Renew spokes as necessary. (See p. 14. Renewing spokes and straightening a wheel. Wheel faults. Checking and replacing bearings.)

Wheel alignment
Check that the wheels rotate smoothly without bumping or wobbling, and adjust if there is any distortion (see p. 14). Stresses on the bicycle—such as a loose spoke or bumping over the kerb—can upset the wheel alignment. On a new machine, check the alignment after about two weeks' use.

Wheel bearings
If a wheel spins roughly when the spindle is hand-held, the wheel bearings and/or the wheel itself need renewing.

Chain
Clean the chain regularly (see p. 11). Check that there is no damage or wear to it, and that the tension is correct. Replace or adjust as necessary.

Basic tool kit

In order to carry out minor repairs and adjustments, a basic tool kit can be kept for use on the road or at home. The kit should consist of the following items:

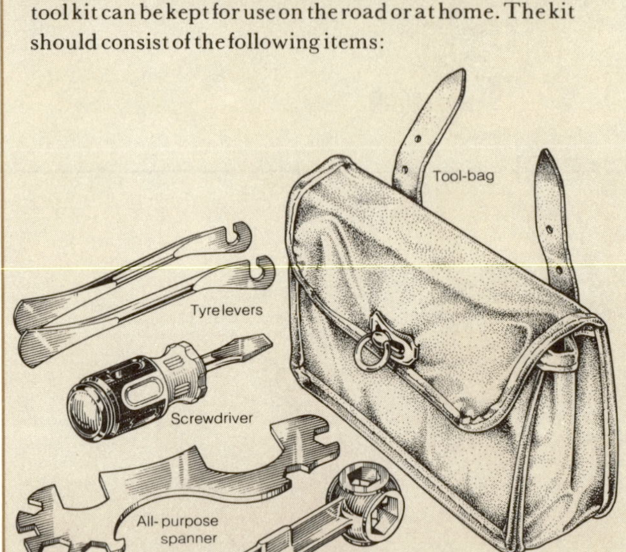

Specialised home tool kit

The following tools and equipment are needed to do one or other of the maintenance or repair jobs described in this book. Some of the items are expensive and may only be used once—if at all—in a lifetime of cycling. It is best, therefore, to buy the more costly items—such as a hide mallet—if and when they are needed. However, such things as oil, cleaning fluid, tyre levers, spanners and so on do not cost very much and should be kept on hand.

Lubricating oil
Anti-rust spray
Paraffin/cleaning fluid
Grease
Rivet extractor
Sprocket extractor
Punch
Hammer
File
Pliers
Wire brush
Rag
Tyre levers
Spoke spanner
Cone spanner
C spanner
Wheel-nut spanner
Straight-edge
Vice
Hardwood block
Hide or plastic mallet
Spoke-key
Small hacksaw
Test lamp
(6 volt bulb)
Bulb holder
Bell wire
Crocodile clips
Ruler
Fine emery cloth

Freewheel sprockets
Check that the teeth are not bent or damaged and that the sprocket does not slip when turning. Replace a damaged or faulty sprocket (see p. 20).

Crank assembly
Ensure that the lock-nut is tight. Replace a bent crank lever, do not try to straighten it. If a cotter-type crank is loose, the cotter pins and/or the crank arm or possibly the axle need renewing. If the assembly turns roughly and with a grating noise instead of freely and smoothly, the bottom-bracket bearings need renewing (see p. 32). To adjust cotterless cranks, a special tool is needed. Adjusting and replacing cotter pins (see p. 33). Removing and greasing a one-piece crankset (see p. 36). Removing a cotterless crankset (see p. 37).

Frame
A bent or broken frame will cause strain or failure in other parts of the bicycle. Replace a faulty frame immediately, or make sure that the new parts—such as a new tube—are welded on at a bicycle repair shop. A frame which is badly bent may make the bicycle pull to one side, making it unsafe to ride.

Front fork
Replace a bent or damaged fork as it will make the cycle veer to one side. Do not attempt to straighten it.

Handlebars
Check that the handlebars are secure, and properly positioned in relation to insertion marks (see p. 28). They should turn freely; if there is any drag or play, adjust the steering head (see p. 28). Replace worn grips or tapes (see p. 29). If there is a harsh or clicking sound, the front fork bearings need replacing (see p. 30).

Saddle
Make sure that the seat clamps are secure and that the seat is properly adjusted to the height of the rider (see p. 28).

Lights
Check that lights are working efficiently, that batteries are sound and not corroding, and that the dynamo is correctly positioned (see p. 38).

Reflectors
Make sure that the rear and spoke reflectors are clean, secure and properly positioned. Replace a damaged unit.

Guarding against rust
Keep all chromed or unpainted metal parts—except wheel rims if the cycle has brake blocks acting on them—lightly oiled to protect them from rust. In wet or wintry conditions, rainwater polluted with industrial waste from the atmosphere, or mud and water flung up from the road, will react with unprotected metal and cause corrosion.

Clean and polish the wheel rims once a fortnight with a chrome cleaner and rag. Apply a proprietary maintenance spray once a month to all moving parts and nuts and bolts.

Lubrication

When a bicycle is in regular use, lubricate the bearings and chain once a fortnight with a cycle oil. Apply a few drops at the places indicated, taking care to keep oil off the tyres and rims.

On some cycles there are no oiling points on the bottom bracket, pedals or hubs. The bearings have been packed with grease during manufacture and need no further attention.

For lubrication of bicycles with variable gears (see p. 16).

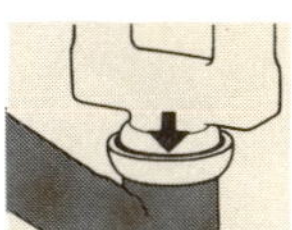

To lubricate the head bearings, turn the cycle upside-down and run oil into the races

Release the brake cable from the lever, hold it upright and run oil between the cable and outer casing

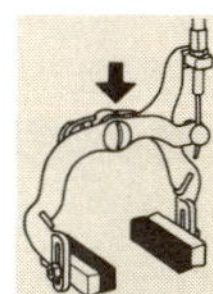

Lubricate the pivot point on each brake caliper; keep oil off the braking surface

Lubricate the free-wheel unit through the oil holes in the face-plate of the gear wheel

With new cycles, grease the wheel hub and ball bearings. To expose the oil hole in the hub, turn the spring clip. After oiling, turn the clip back again

Trickle oil over the links while turning the chain slowly. Wipe off surplus oil

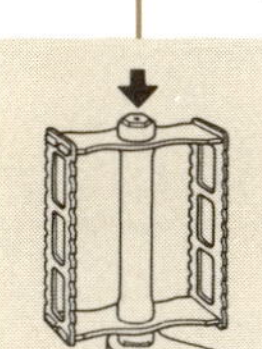

Apply oil through the hole in the end cap on the pedal plate

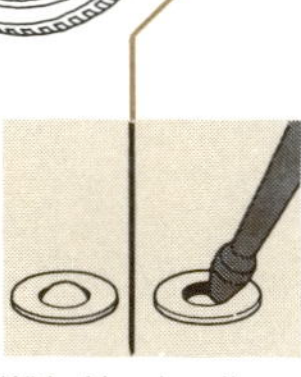

With old cycles, oil the bottom-bracket bearings through the spring-loaded ball located on top of the bracket

ROD BRAKES
Oil the lever bearings, the stirrup guides on both brakes and all pivot points (see p. 24).

Chains

Testing and fitting

Testing a chain: fitting a new one

Grit, lack of oil or wrong tensioning will cause chain wear. In use, a worn chain makes a grating sound.

Each link of the chain is made up of two side plates riveted at one end to a central roller. Generally, the ends of the chain are joined by a connecting link, the closed end of which must face the direction of travel. The endless Derailleur gear chain has no connecting link.

Most new chains need shortening by removing one or two surplus links. This is easiest with a rivet extractor, but a fine punch and hammer will do. Follow the same procedure to shorten an old chain. Replace worn sprockets (see p. 20) with new ones when fitting a new chain.

Materials: new chain; paraffin.
Tools: rivet extractor, or a fine punch and a hammer; pliers; spanner; wire brush.

CHAIN WEAR

Worn Some of the chain links can be seen to ride over the top of the chain-wheel teeth

Unworn The chain 'beds down' between the chain-wheel teeth without any lifting

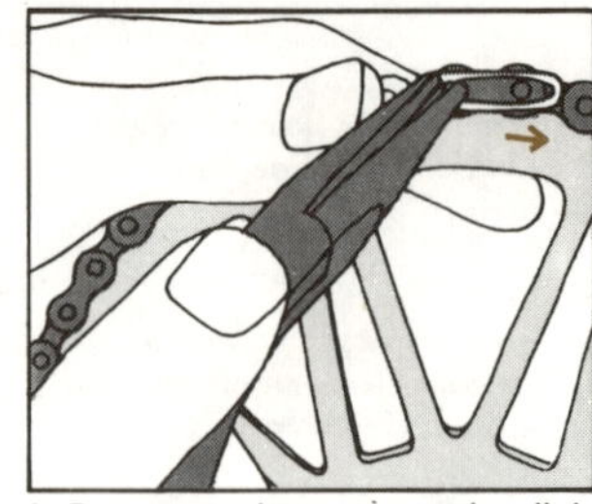

1 Remove the connecting-link spring clip by closing the pliers across one of the rivet heads and the ends of the clip

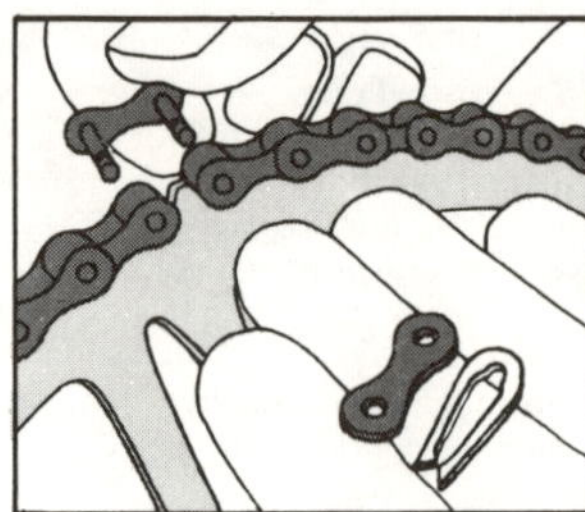

2 With the clip off, withdraw the end plate and slide the main body of the connecting link from the ends of the chain

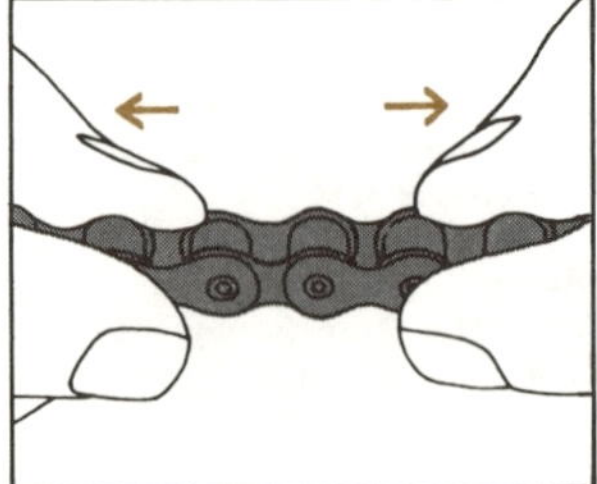

3 Pull two adjacent chain links in opposite directions. If there is much play between them a new chain must be fitted

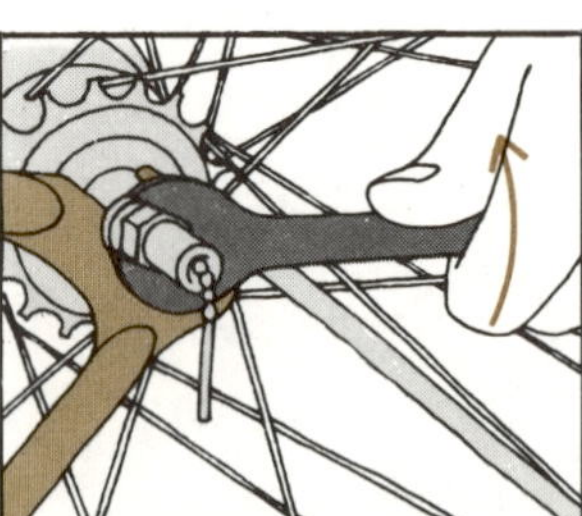

4 To allow full adjustment of the chain, loosen the rear-wheel nuts and move the wheel forward as far as it will safely go

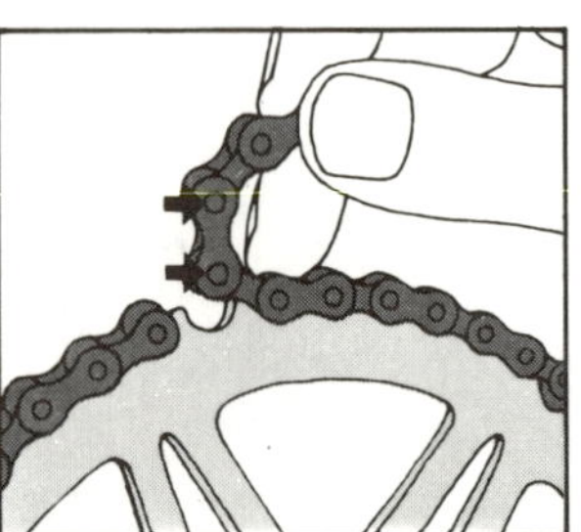

5 Fit the chain tightly over the two sprockets. The arrows indicate the rivets that must be removed to make the chain fit

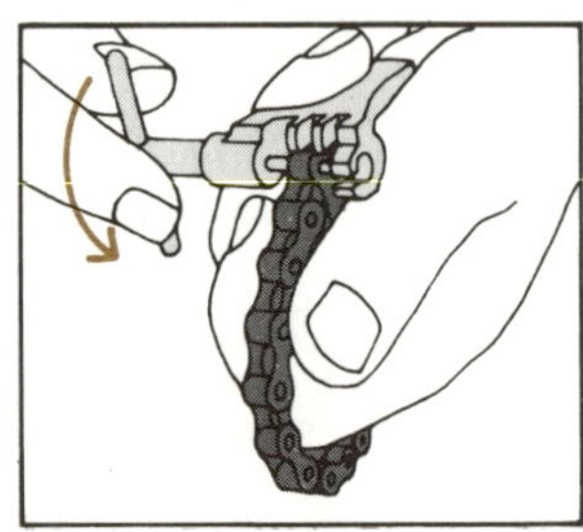

6 With the rivet in the rivet-extractor jaws, give the handle six full down-turns. Make sure to hold the extractor steady and level

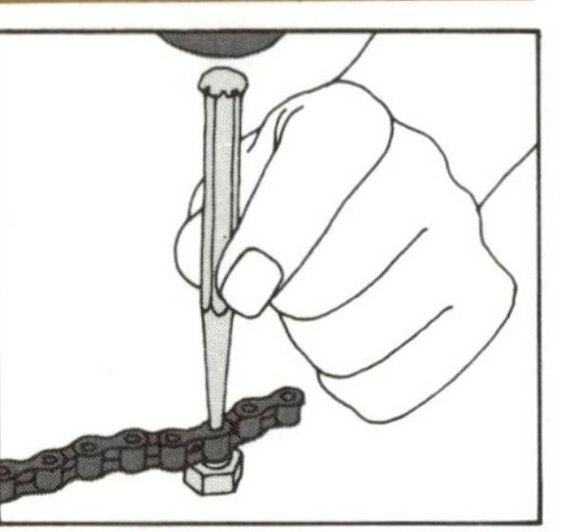

7 If you have no extractor, put the rivet over the centre of a small nut and tap the rivet flat. Drive it out with a fine punch

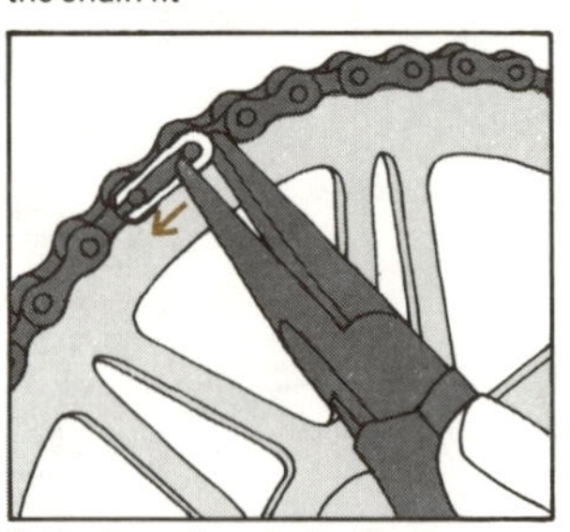

8 Replace the chain. Fit the connecting link, placing the clip over one rivet and pressing it over the other into the rivet grooves

9 Adjust the rear wheel to give the chain $\frac{1}{2}$ in. (13 mm) of free play. Position the wheel centrally and tighten the securing nuts

Chains

Cleaning and fitting

Cleaning a chain

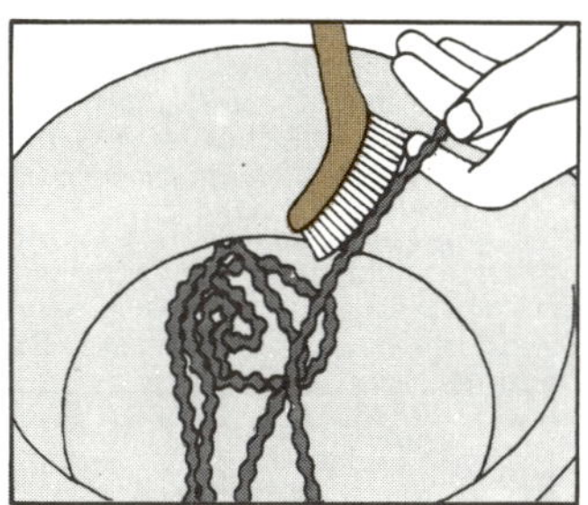

1 Soak the chain overnight in a bowl of paraffin. Then remove sand and grit with a wire brush or an old toothbrush

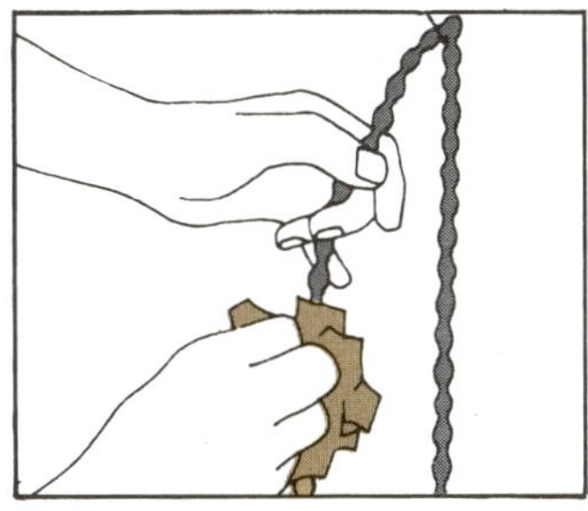

2 Hang up the chain to let the paraffin run off. Dry it with a clean rag, ensuring that no material is caught in the links

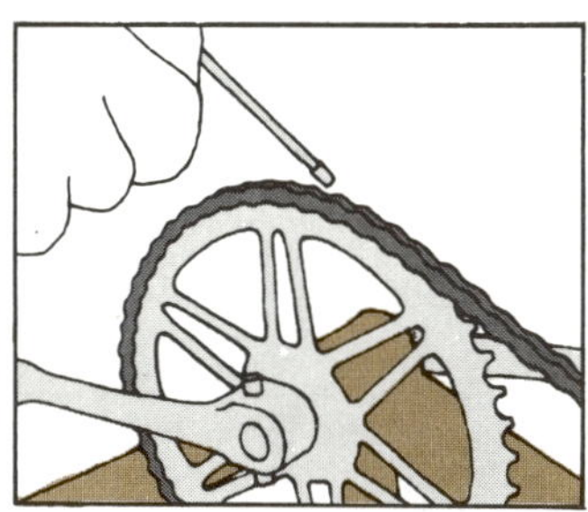

3 Refit the chain, adjust the tension, and oil each link with a proprietary cycle lubricant

Fitting an endless chain

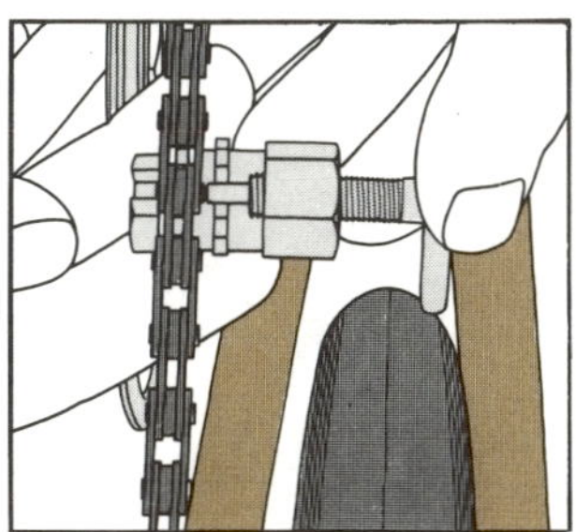

1 Move the rear wheel as far forward as it will go without taking it off. Using a rivet extractor, connect the extractor on to a chain link and turn the handle six times

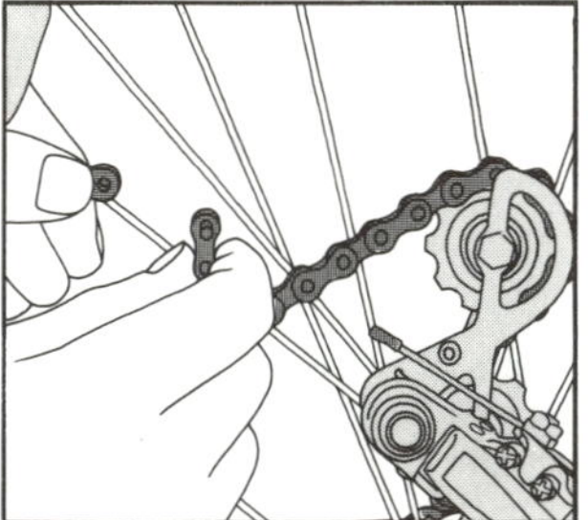

2 Feed the chain around the chain wheel and Derailleur and link the chain together. A link or two may need to be taken out to allow for the required adjustment

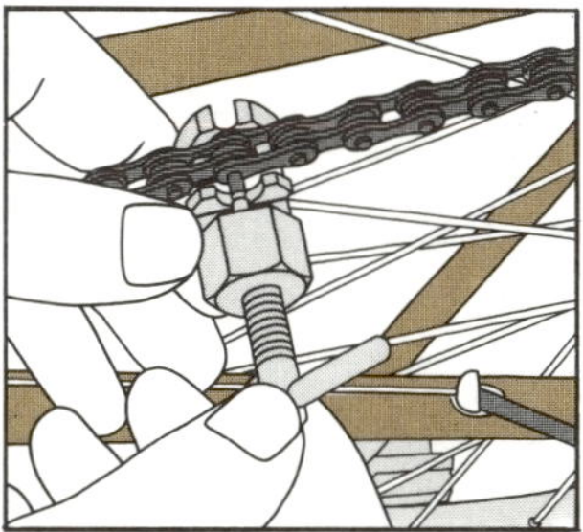

3 To reconnect the chain, slide the open link into the adjacent link, with the pin protruding. Use a rivet extractor to push the pin through both links, by turning the handle

Valves

Valves – checking for faults

There are three main types of tyre valve: the Woods and Schrader, which are normal pressure valves; and the Presta, or high-pressure valve used on most sports cycles. The Woods and Schrader valves can be repaired if faulty, but a faulty Presta valve, and the inner tube, will have to be replaced.

To replace a faulty Schrader valve, use the special key-like tool provided. Turn the key anti-clockwise to remove the valve from the valve stem. To fit a new valve turn the key clockwise.

To replace a faulty Woods valve, remove the dustcap and retaining nut and lift out the valve. Insert the new valve into the body then replace the retaining nut and tighten it fully. Finally, replace the dustcap and twist it firmly home.

VALVES: HIGH-PRESSURE AND NORMAL PRESSURE

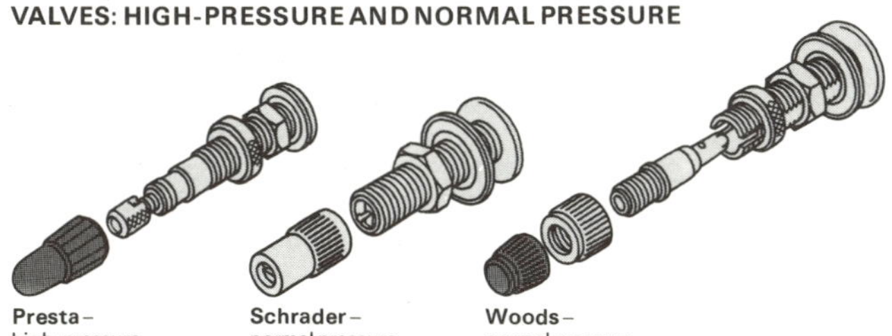

CHECKING FOR LEAKY VALVES

To check whether a valve is leaking, lift the wheel from the ground and turn it until the valve is at the top and easy to hand. Remove the dustcap from the valve and submerge the valve in an egg-cup, or a similar container, filled with water.

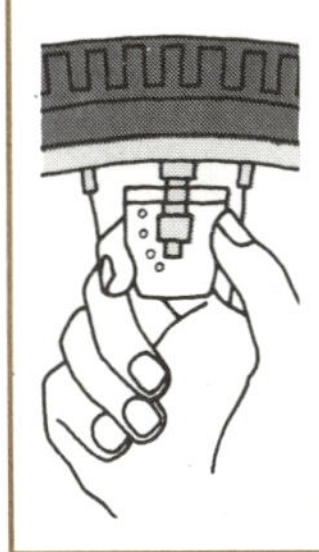

A leak will be shown by the presence of bubbles in the water

Wheels

Valves and inner tubes

Mending a puncture

A flat tyre may be caused by a faulty valve or a punctured inner tube. Check the valve first. If it is sound, note the position of any flints or nails that may have damaged the tube before removing the tyre. After removing the tube, check that the rim tape is in good condition and covering the spoke nipples.

To detect a puncture without using water, move the inflated tube along slowly close to your ear or lips. If air is escaping from an old patch, remove the patch using a piece of glass-paper to remove any surplus glue. Then clean with petrol and a rag and put on a new patch.

Materials: puncture-repair outfit containing an indelible pencil, glass-paper or an abrasive stick for cleaning the tube, rubber solution, rubber patches and French chalk; petrol.
Tools: three tyre levers.

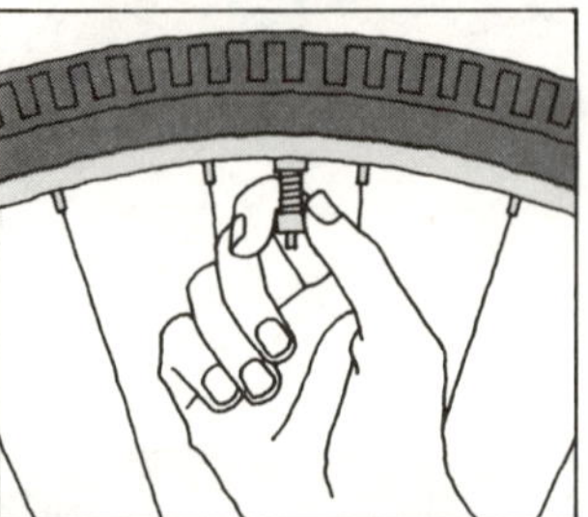

1 Unscrew the nut that retains the valve assembly and withdraw the valve from the inner-tube stem

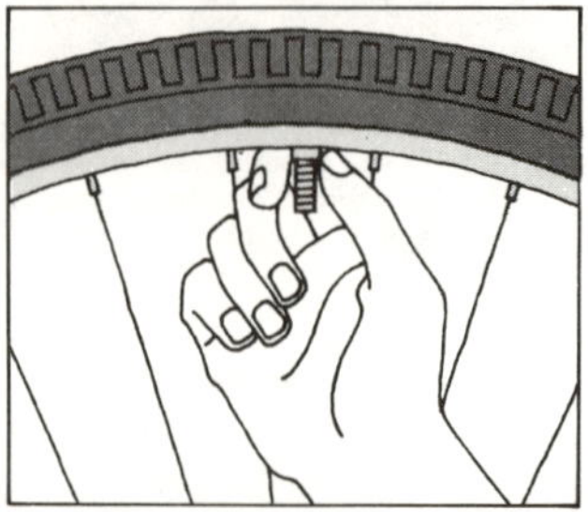

2 Remove the lock-ring and push part of the valve stem up inside the wheel rim to free the cover

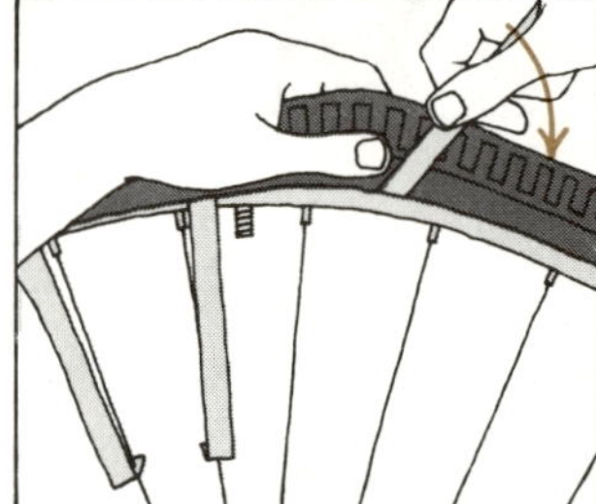

3 Insert the levers between the rim and tyre. Lever the tyre off, hooking each lever in turn round a spoke

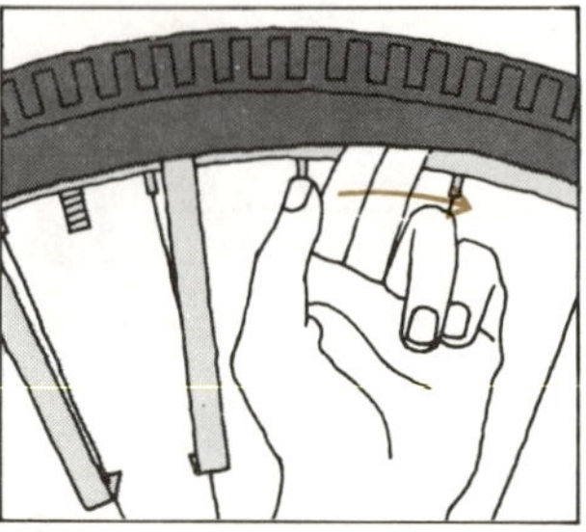

4 When a quarter of the tyre has been levered off, run two fingers round the rim to free the rest of the tyre

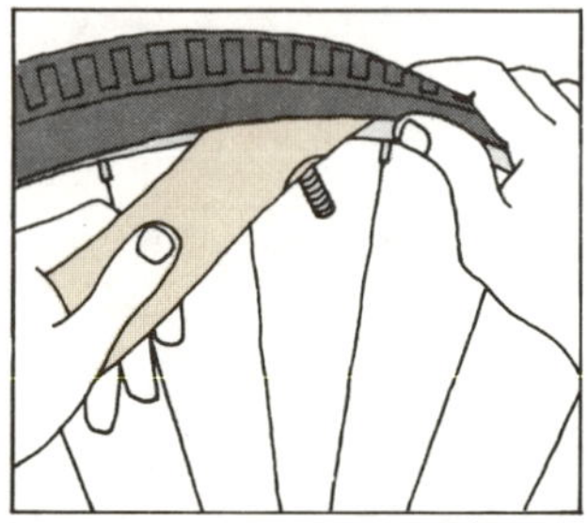

5 With one edge of the cover removed, draw the tube out. Press it to the rim to ease it past the brake blocks

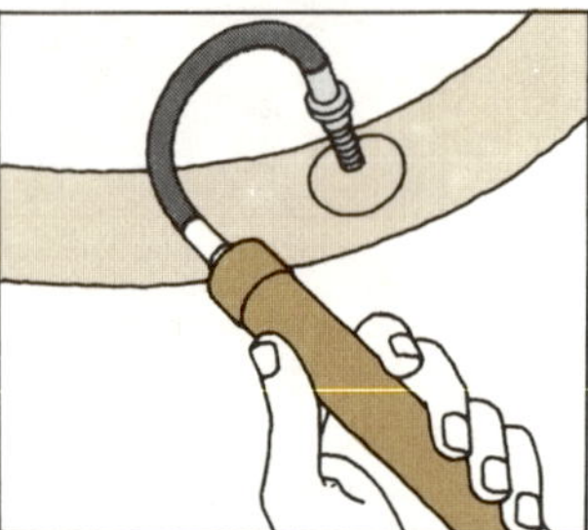

6 Replace the valve and its retaining nut and inflate the tube just sufficiently for it to adopt its natural shape

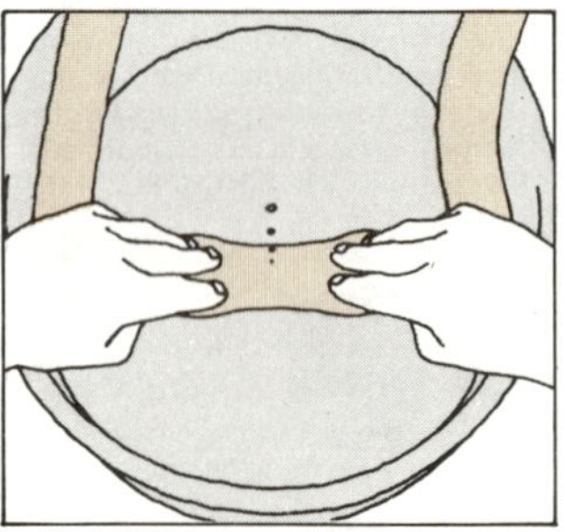

7 Pass the tube through a bowl of water, stretching it slightly to enlarge any small punctures

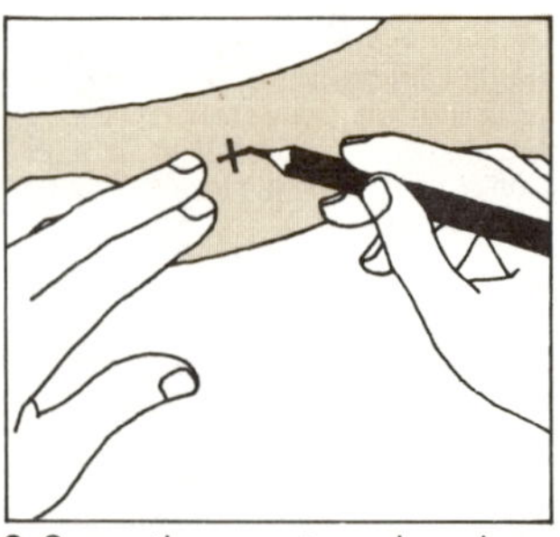

8 Once the puncture has been located, mark its position with the indelible pencil in the kit

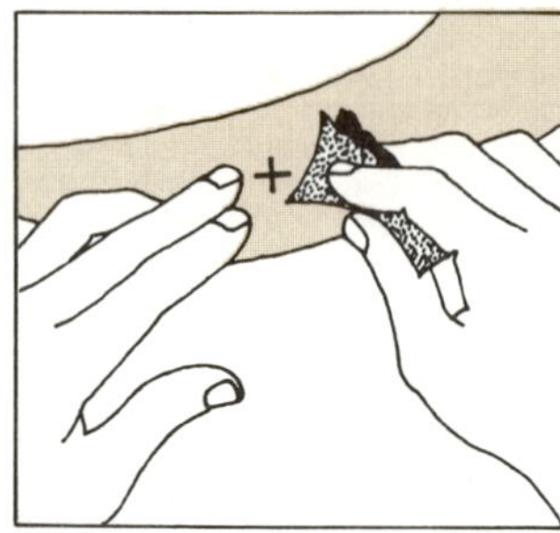

9 Deflate the tube and clean the area with glass-paper, a moistened abrasive stick or a petrol-soaked cloth

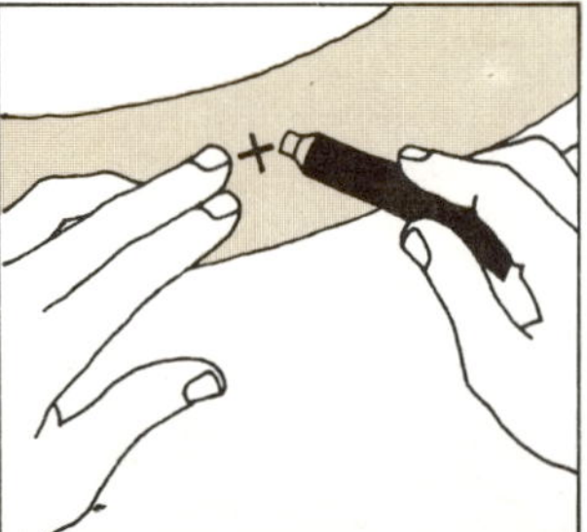

10 Spread the adhesive thinly over the surface around the mark and leave it until it is practically dry

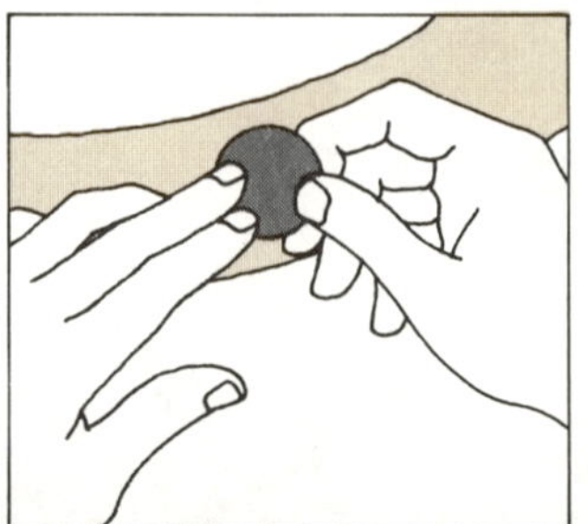

11 Peel off the backing from a patch and press the patch, tacky side down, firmly over the puncture

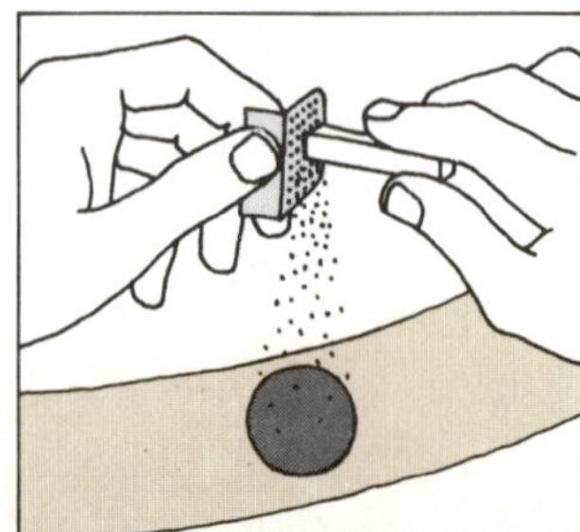

12 Dry any surplus adhesive with French chalk. If solid chalk is provided in the kit, powder it on the grater

Fitting a new rim tape

A rim tape is fitted to protect the inner tube from possible puncture by the spoke nipples. When a tyre and tube have to be removed for any reason, it is as well to examine the tape for signs of misplacement or deterioration. This often starts with rust stains, developing eventually into fraying or splitting.

There are two types of tapes—one made of a thin webbing material, the other of rubber. Rubber tapes, used mainly on sports cycles, cost more but are less trouble to fit. They must be bought to fit the wheel, whereas webbing tapes are adjustable. Tools are not needed in either case.

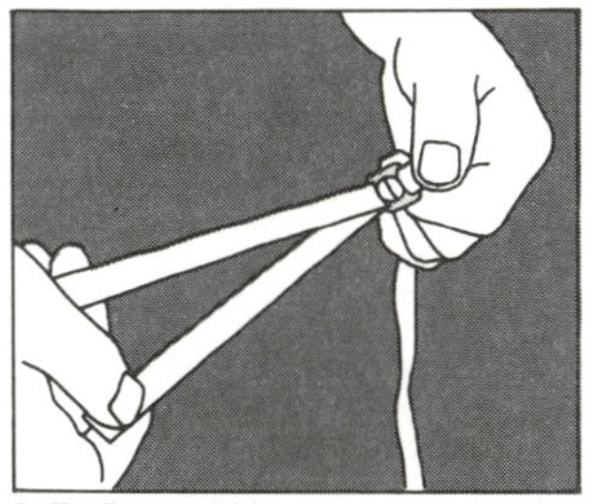

1 To fit a webbing tape, open it with the convex side of the eye downwards and pass the free end through the slot from the top

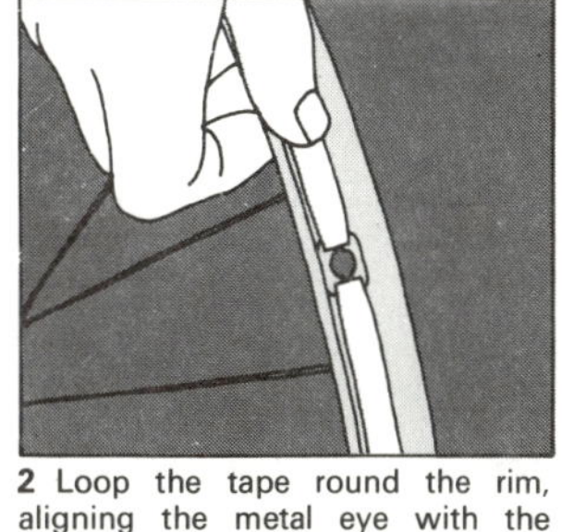

2 Loop the tape round the rim, aligning the metal eye with the wheel-rim valve hole. Make sure that the tape is not twisted

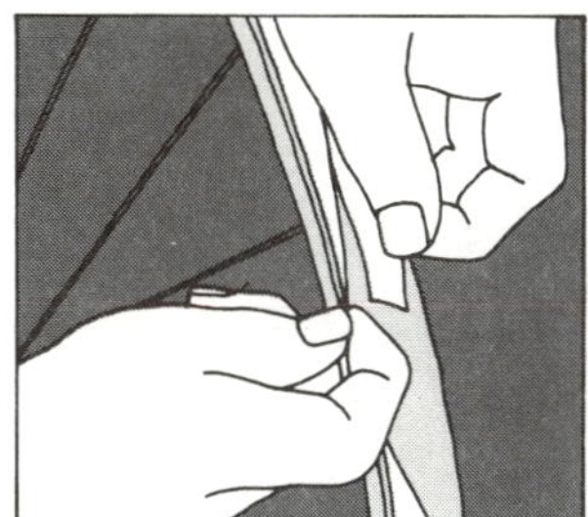

3 Keeping the eye and valve hole aligned, draw the tape tight. Tuck the surplus material under the main run of the rest of the tape

4 Fit a rubber tape convex side downwards. Align the tape's valve hole with the wheel-rim valve hole, then feed the tape round the rim

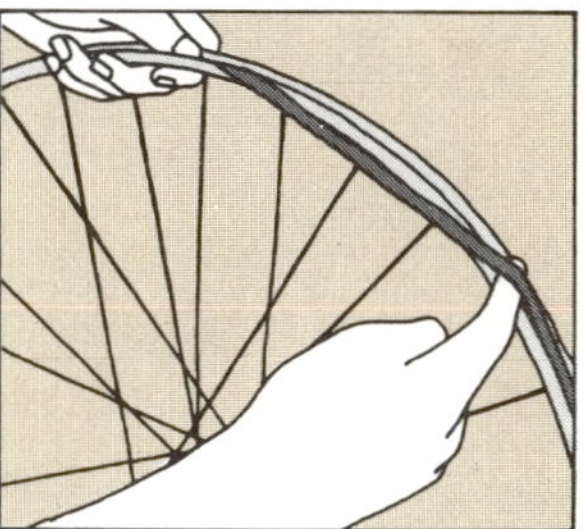

5 To avoid twisting the tape, draw a finger under it as it springs over the rim. See that it sits centrally in the well of the rim

Refitting a tyre and tube

1 Slip one entire side of the tyre over an edge of the wheel rim, taking care as you do so not to push the rim tape out of position

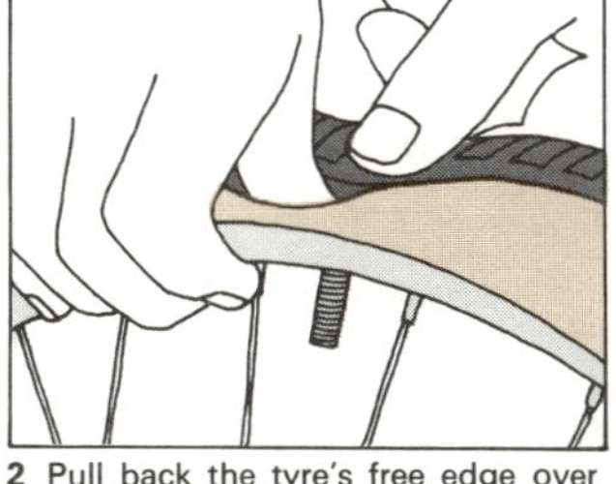

2 Pull back the tyre's free edge over the valve hole in the rim and insert the valve stem; then draw the tyre back over the inner tube

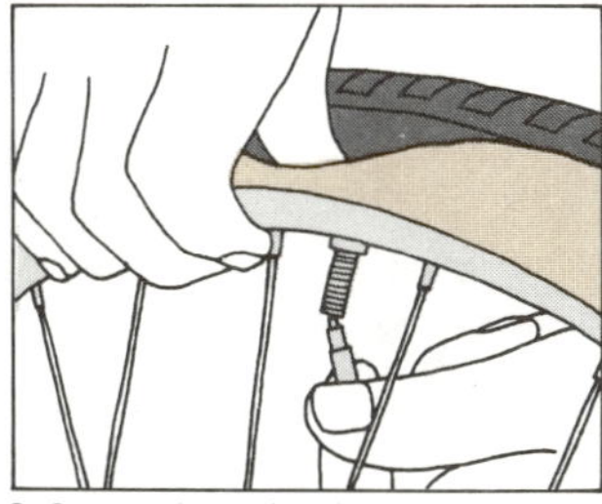

3 Screw the valve lock-ring finger-tight. Replace the valve, checking the rubber in older-type valves, and tighten the valve retaining nut

4 Inflate the inner tube enough to give it its natural shape. Avoid over-inflation, as this makes it difficult to refit the tyre

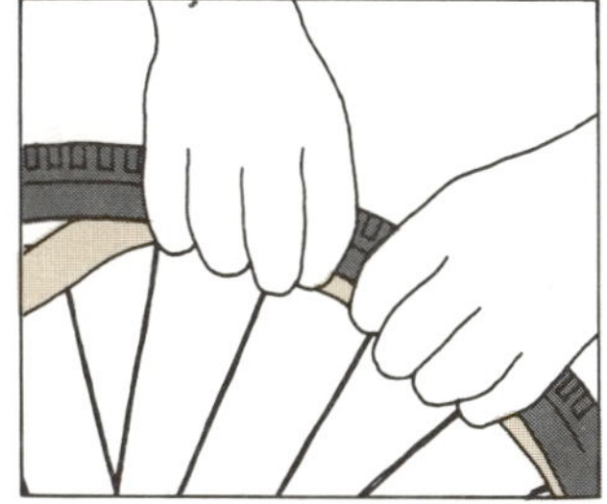

5 Roll the tube into the centre of the rim well. Adjust the fitted edge of the tyre if necessary to ensure that the tube is positioned correctly

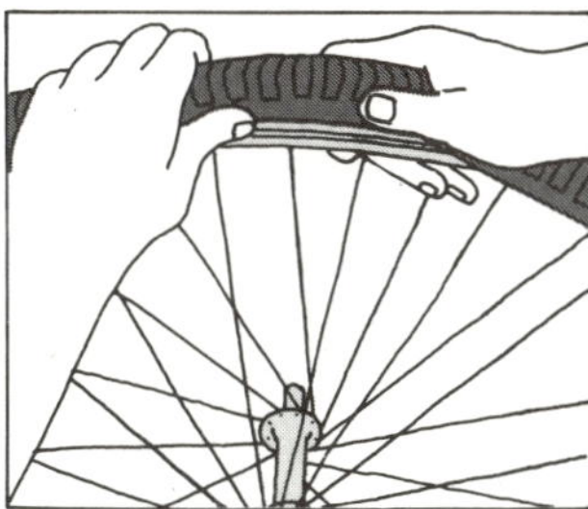

6 Draw the free edge of the tyre into the rim well, finishing with a small section of tyre overlapping the rim across the valve stem

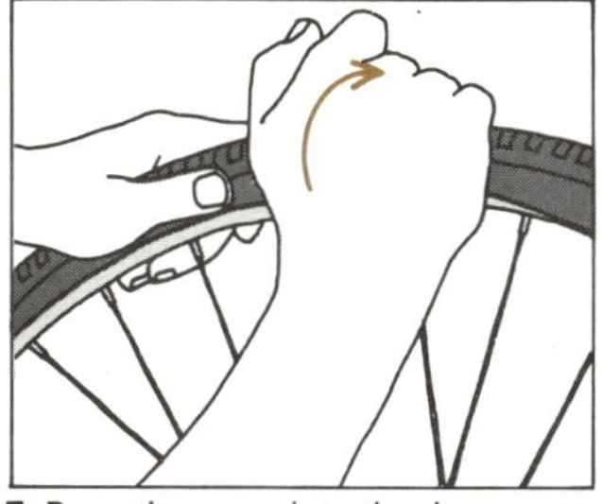

7 Press the cover into the rim centre, working from both sides towards the area still to be fitted. Roll the last part on with the balls of the thumbs

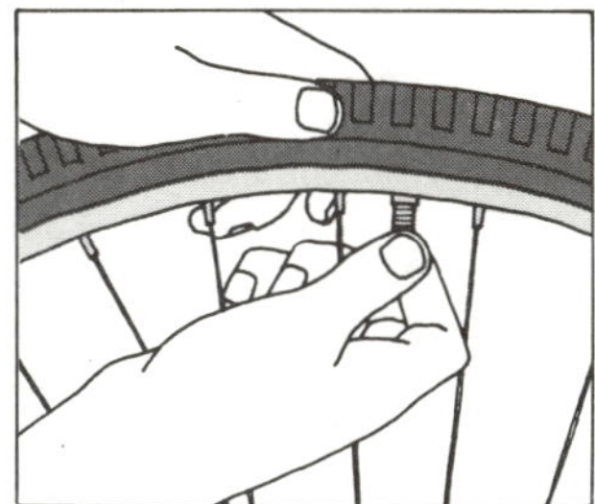

8 Loosen the valve stem lock-ring and push the stem into the rim. Pull the stem out again, tighten the lock-ring and inflate the tyre

Renewing spokes and straightening a wheel

Just one faulty spoke can throw a wheel out of true, causing erratic braking and a tendency to wobble. Spokes are fitted in alternate directions on each side of the hub. Below, in part, are the spoke arrangements on a front and a rear wheel. If several spokes are missing, it is essential to 'lace in' the new ones correctly.

A wheel may be out of true in two ways (see right). A radial distortion makes the rim uneven, with the hub slightly off-centre, and can give a bumpy ride. A lateral distortion causes side-to-side movement.

Most such wheel faults are caused by riding over kerbstones, potholes or on uneven road surfaces. Sometimes faults occur through not noticing a bent or broken spoke. Spokes should be checked for faults once a week.

Materials: replacement spokes of correct length; nipples.
Tools: sprocket extractor; screwdriver; chalk; spoke-key; straight-edge; file.

IDENTIFYING DISTORTION

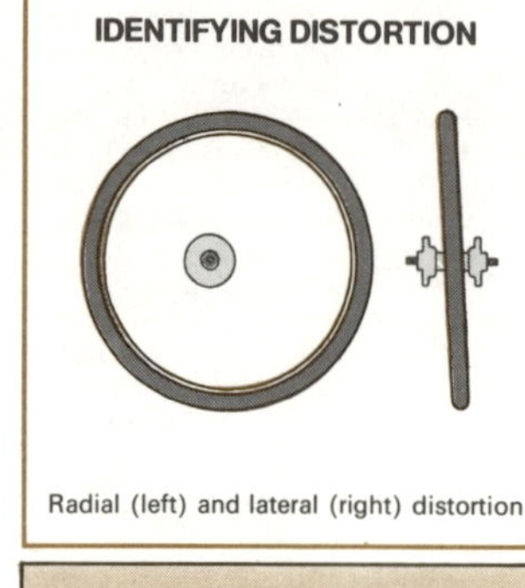

Radial (left) and lateral (right) distortion

Front wheel The spokes radiate from the hub and hold in position the rim of the wheel

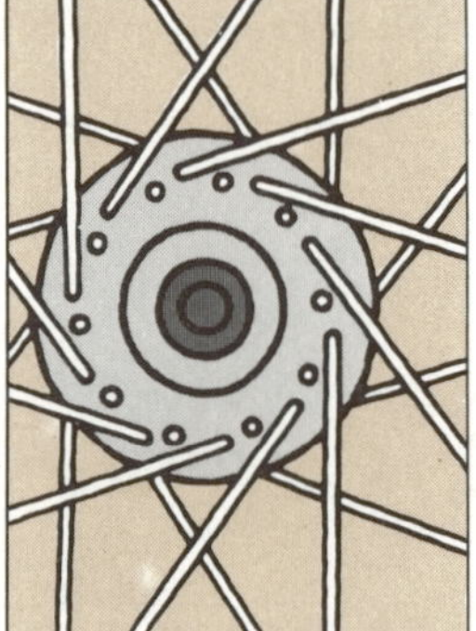

Rear wheel As with the front spokes, the rear spokes screw into the rim and are adjustable

1 Remove the gear-sprocket on the right-hand side of the wheel to replace a broken or damaged spoke or spokes. Use a sprocket extractor

2 Remove the tyre and replace the wheel. Take out both ends of a broken spoke; unscrew the nipple to release a bent spoke

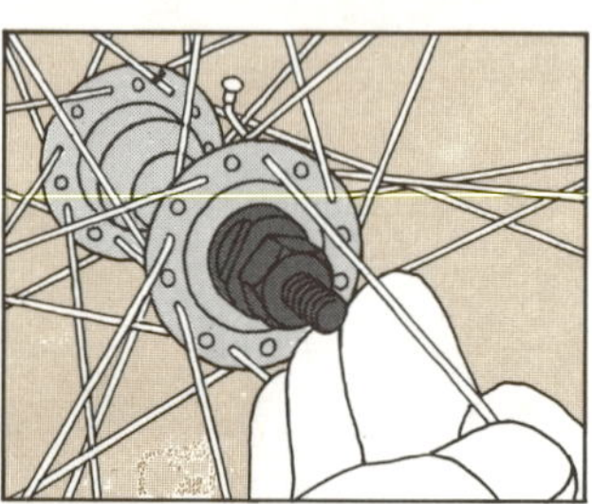

3 Feed a new spoke through the hub hole. The head must be on the opposite side of the hub to the spoke-heads on either side of it

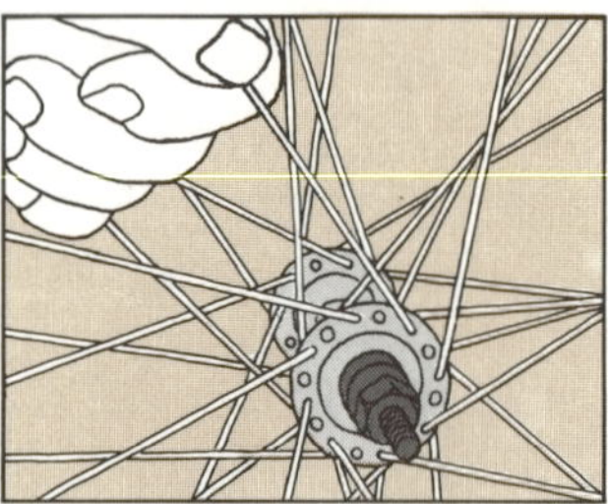

4 Draw out and swing up the spoke to the wheel-rim hole, making sure that it laces across the correct number of fitted spokes

5 Fit the spoke through the rim hole and screw the spoke nipple on to the threaded end. Tension the spoke with a screwdriver

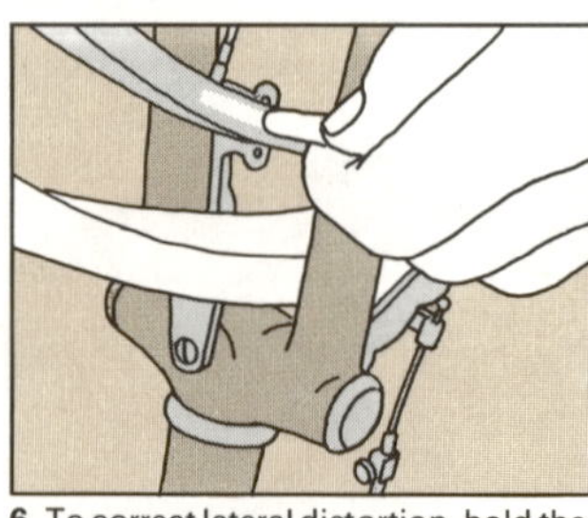

6 To correct lateral distortion, hold the chalk close to the rim, spin the wheel and then mark the spot where the chalk touches

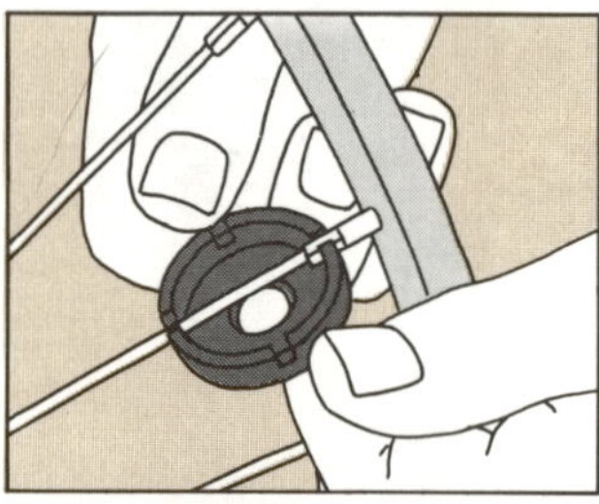

7 Using the spoke-key, tighten only the spokes which lead to the opposite side of the hub. Adjust half a turn at a time until the wheel is true

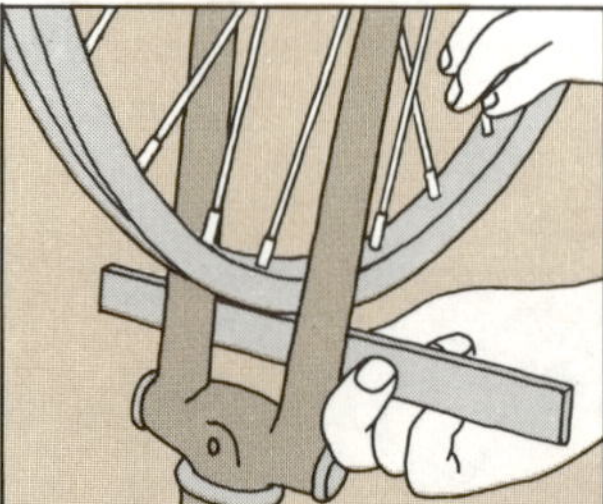

8 To correct radial distortion, remove the mudguard and place a straight-edge across the forks column at right angles to the rim. Spin the wheel

9 Raise the edge so that it just touches out-of-true rim areas. Mark those areas with chalk and tighten all spokes at these points

10 Finally, check to see if there are any spokes protruding from their nipple-heads. File them off flush with the nipples

Checking and replacing bearings

Wheel-bearing wear is caused by dirt, lack of oil, or over-tightening. It can be felt as a roughness if the wheel is spun while the spindle is hand-held. The ball bearings and cones are most likely to be affected; the two cups, generally integral parts of the hub, seldom wear. If they do, replace the wheel.

Materials: new cones and bearings as necessary; grease; paraffin.
Tools: spanners, including cone spanner; vice.

Wheel nut
Lock-nut
Fixed cone
Ball bearings
Hub

Bearing cup
Ball bearings
Adjustable cone
Lock-nut
Wheel nut

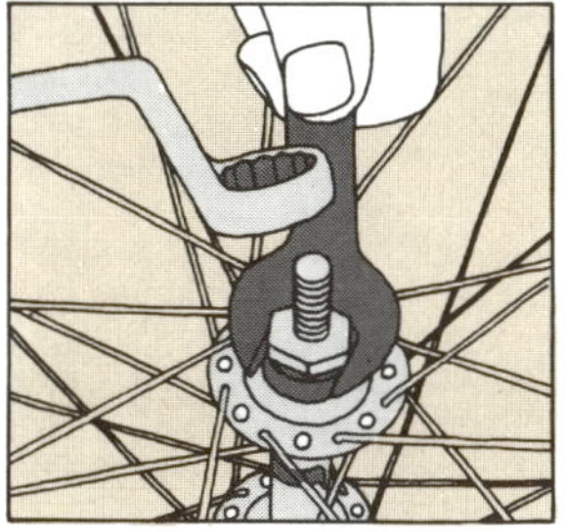

1 Remove the wheel nuts and the wheel. If it is the rear one, remove the chain from the sprocket

2 Holding the spindle in a vice and the adjustable cone with a spanner, undo the lock-nut

3 Unscrew the cone. It should be only finger-tight, but a cone spanner may be needed

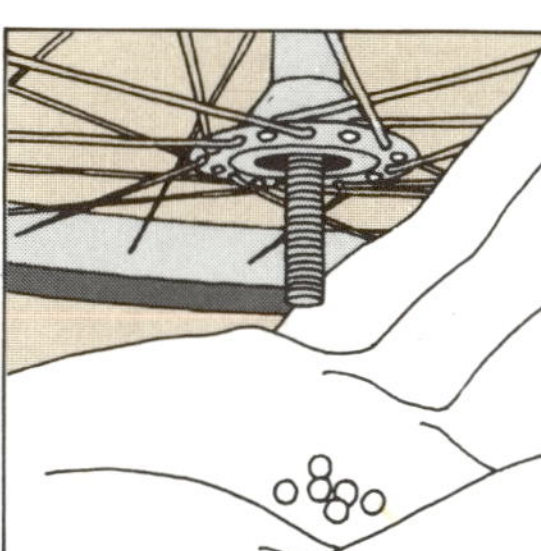

4 Undo the vice, with the spindle in position. Invert the wheel to release the ball bearings

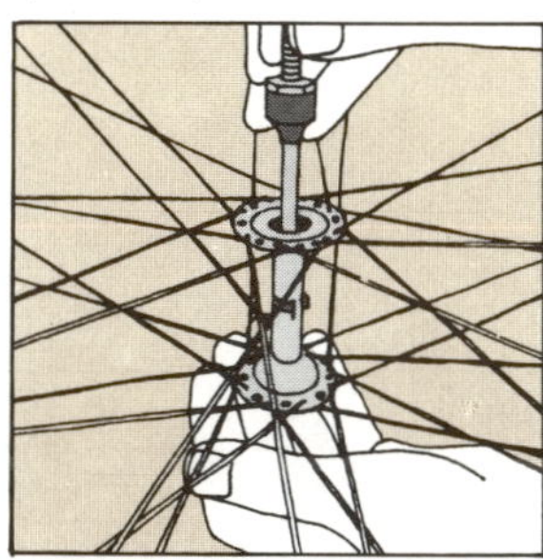

5 Draw out the spindle and shake out the other ball bearings from beneath the wheel hub

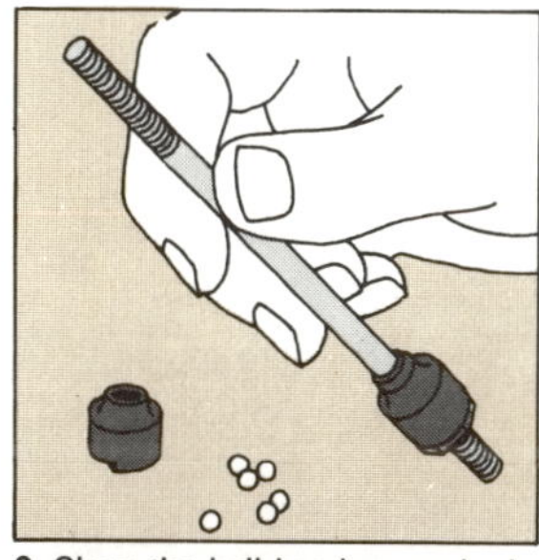

6 Clean the ball bearings and adjustable cone with paraffin. Replace any parts that are worn

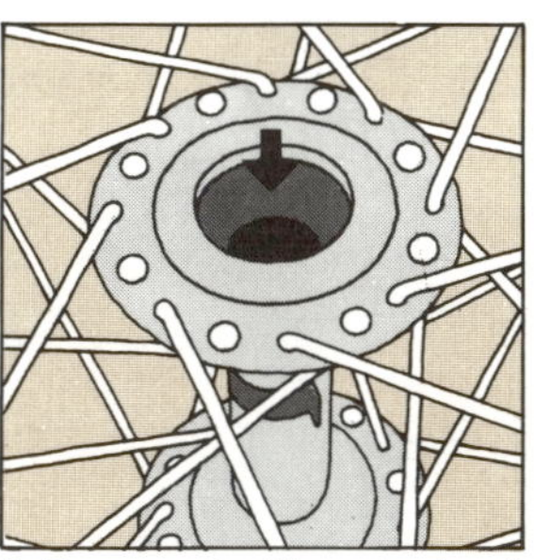

7 Remove all old or hardened grease from the hub cups: clean and check for signs of wear

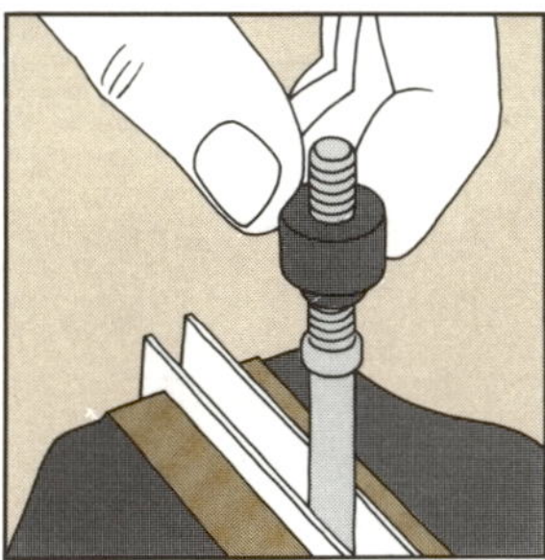

8 Place two pieces of cardboard in vice and clamp the spindle between them. Replace fixed cone

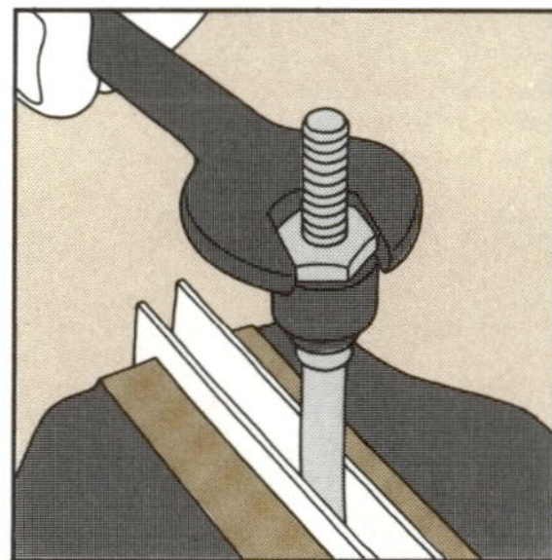

9 Tighten the cone down to the stop. Replace and tighten the lock-nut if one was fitted

10 Loosely position the spindle, grease the hub cups, and fit the ball bearings to one cup

11 Reverse the wheel, hold the spindle in the vice, and refit the other ball bearings and cone

12 Adjust the cone so that the wheel turns under the weight of the valve. Replace the lock-nut

Renewing a trigger-control gear cable

Hub gears are generally controlled by a trigger on the handlebars. This seldom gives trouble if oiled regularly, but the connecting cable may wear and need replacing. A new cable, complete with outer casing, can be bought from any cycle dealer. Fitting is straightforward if the stages are followed correctly. Oil the rear hub fortnightly—the oil hole is generally protected by a sprung cap—and occasionally oil the cable pulley.

Materials: new trigger-control cable; oil.
Tool: screwdriver.

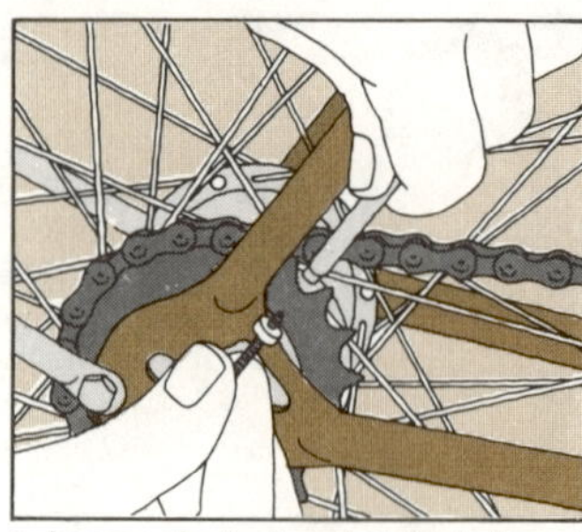

1 Loosen the lock-nut at the hub end and separate the cable adjuster and hub toggle chain

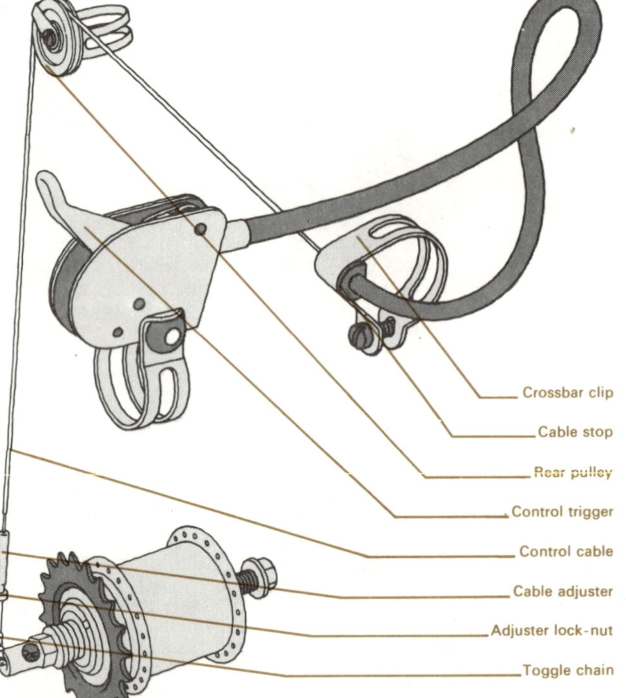

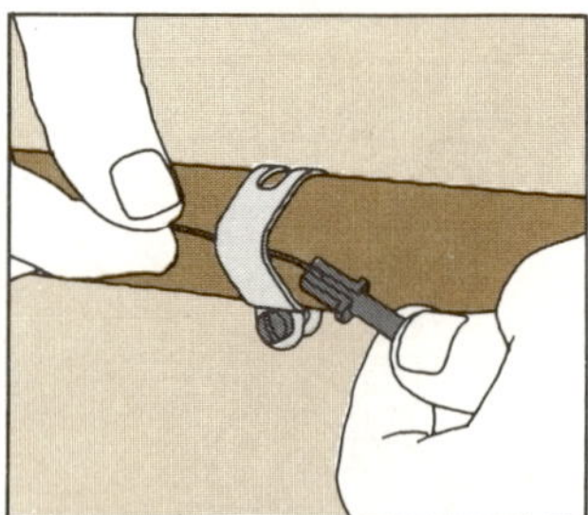

2 Take the gear cable and stop from the clip. The stop is split, so the cable can be slipped out

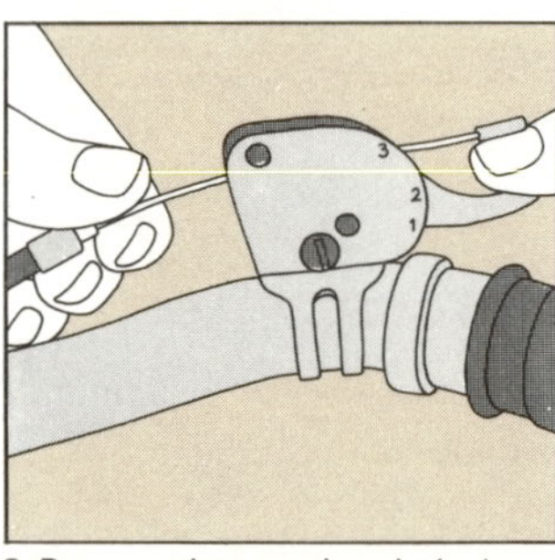

3 Depress trigger and push the inner cable towards the trigger to free the nipple. Then draw out the cable

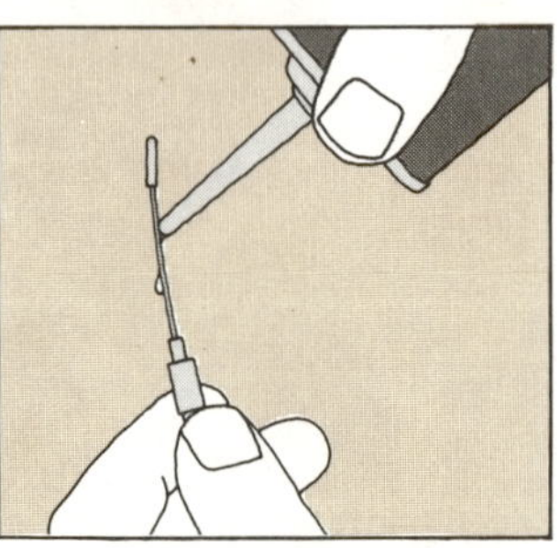

4 Before fitting the new cable, lightly lubricate the control end of the inner cable with bicycle oil

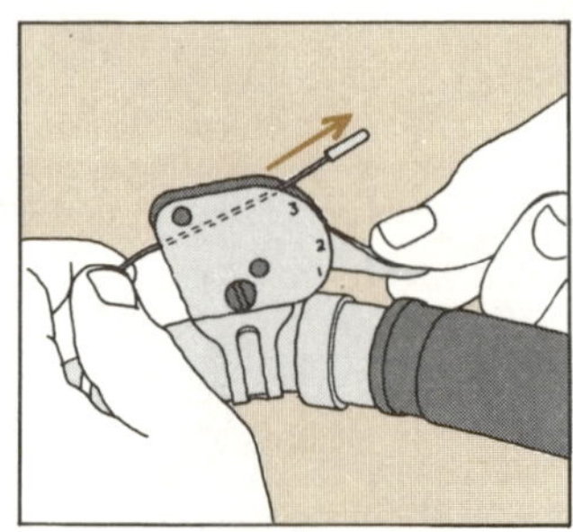

5 Keep the trigger depressed and push the cable nipple through the front of the unit

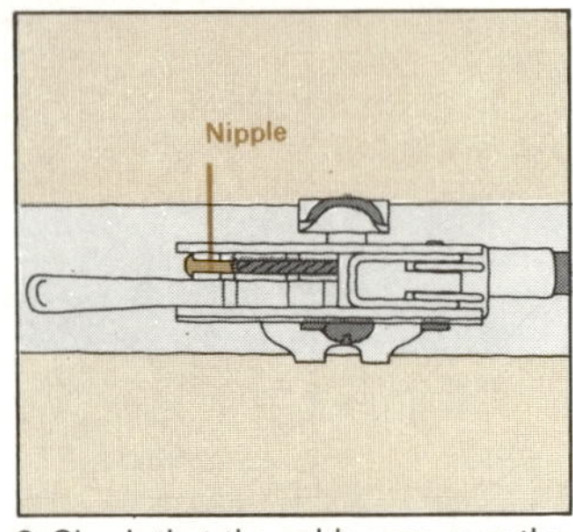

6 Check that the cable runs over the trigger-control slot and that the nipple is located correctly

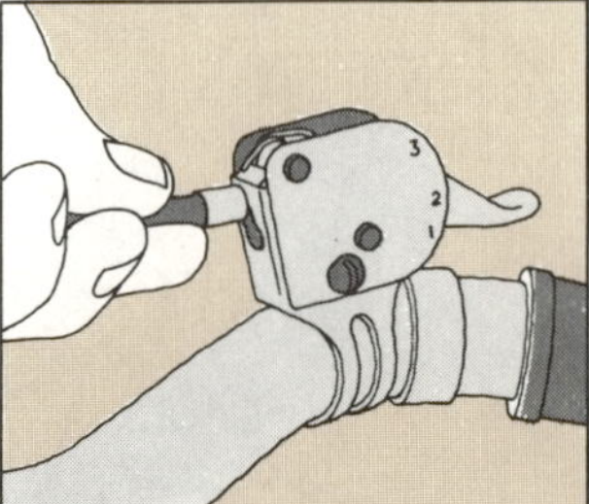

7 Slip the outer cable stop into the wider part of the slot, then slide the cable upwards

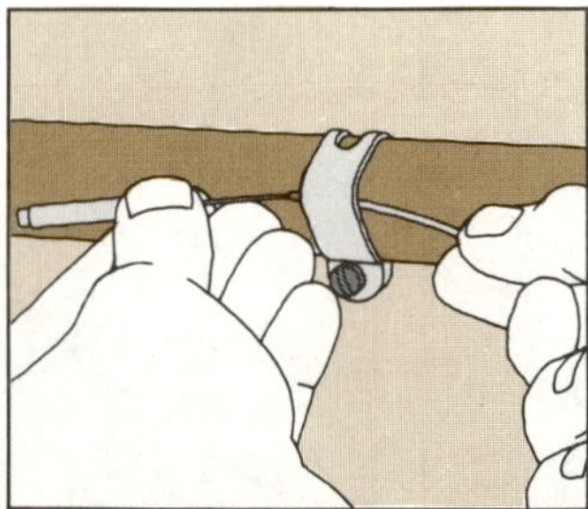

8 Slide the cable adjuster through the crossbar clip before fitting the outer cable stop

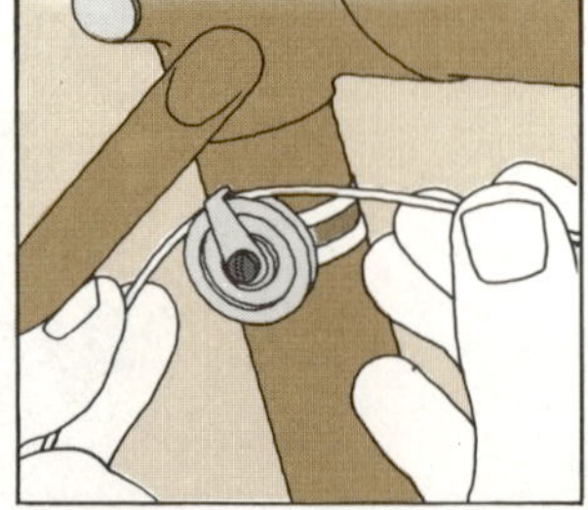

9 Check that the rear pulley rotates freely, apply oil, then feed the inner cable over it

10 Tighten the toggle by cranking it at 90 degrees to the hub spindle. Finally, unwind half a turn

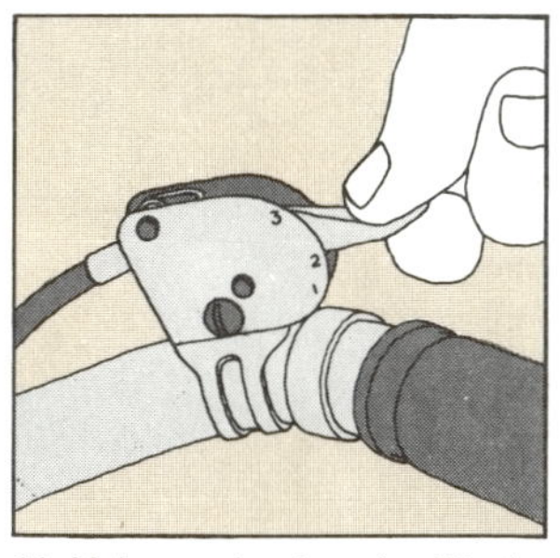

11 Make sure the trigger is still in the number two position before connecting the cable to the chain

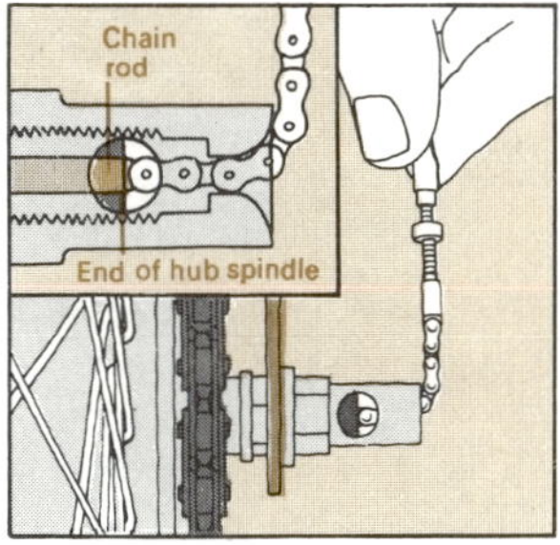

12 Turn the adjuster until the end of the chain rod is level with the end of the hub spindle; tighten lock-nut

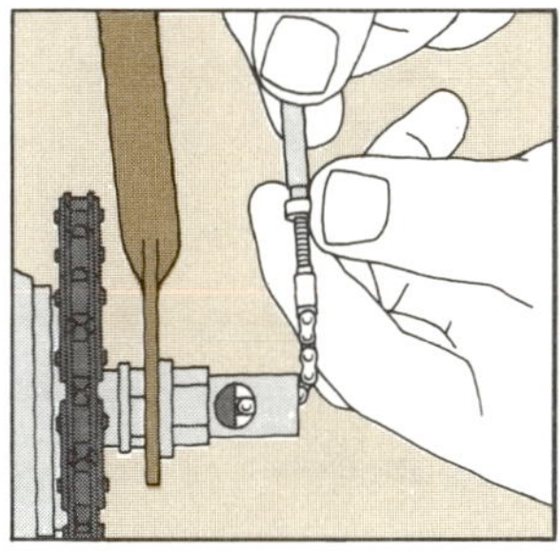

13 After adjustment, set the gear in third position and screw the adjuster lock-nut upwards

Renewing a twist-grip control gear cable

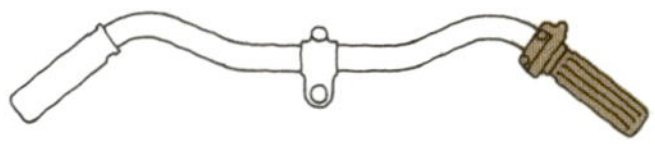

Twist-grip gear changes are nowadays often fitted to cycles which have Sturmey Archer hub gears. Before replacing a cable, the unit has to be removed from the handlebars; but in other respects the job is similar to replacing a trigger-control unit. Take particular note of how the components are positioned, as correct assembly is essential for smooth working.

Materials: twist-grip control cable.
Tool: screwdriver.

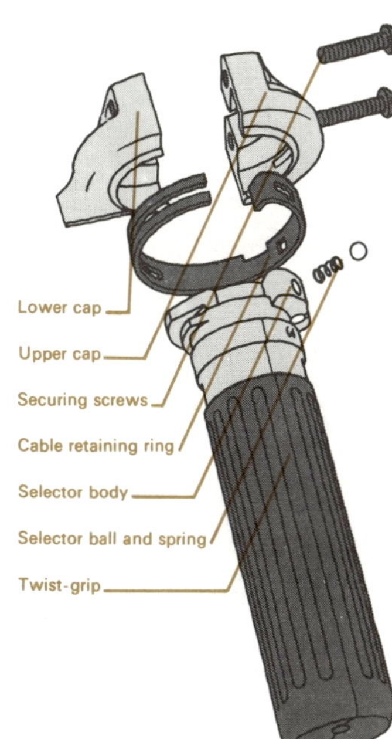

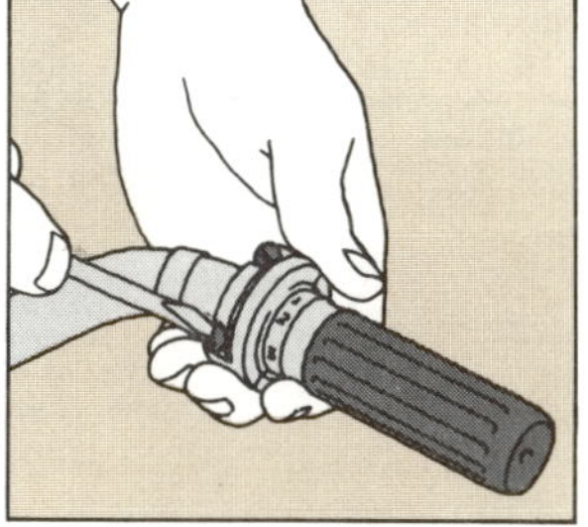

1 Undo the twist-grip's two securing screws one full turn and remove the grip from the handlebars

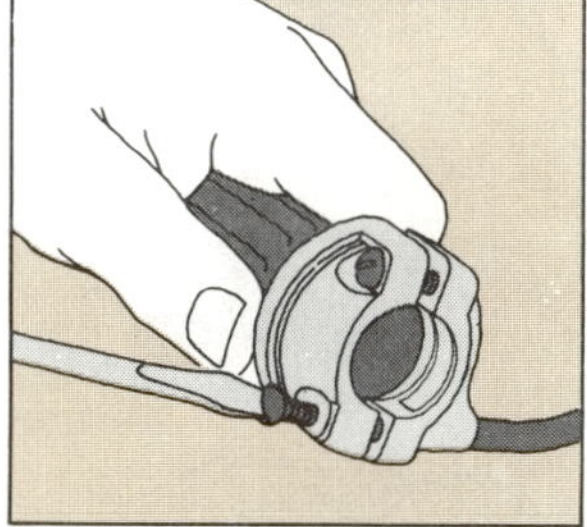

2 With the control removed, start dismantling it by taking out the two securing screws

3 Holding the twist-grip with one hand, lift the upper cap of the clamp off the body of the grip

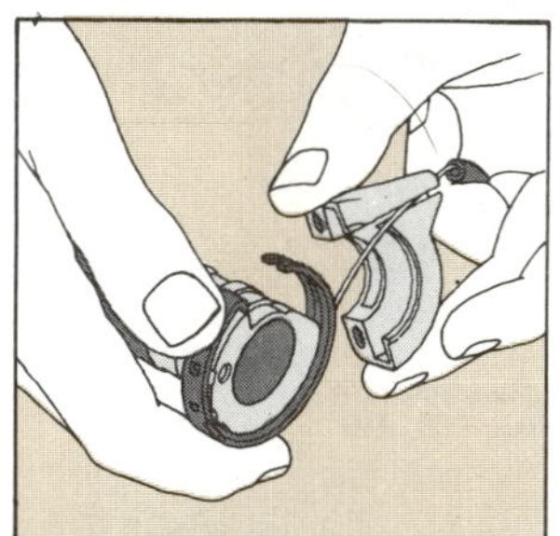

4 Slide the cap's lower half down the cable. Slip the cable out through the slot in the cap's side

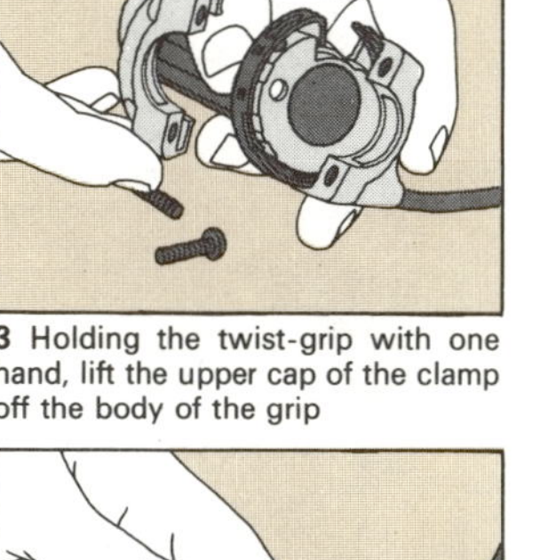

5 Take the cable retaining ring off the grip and slide the cable out through the slot in the ring

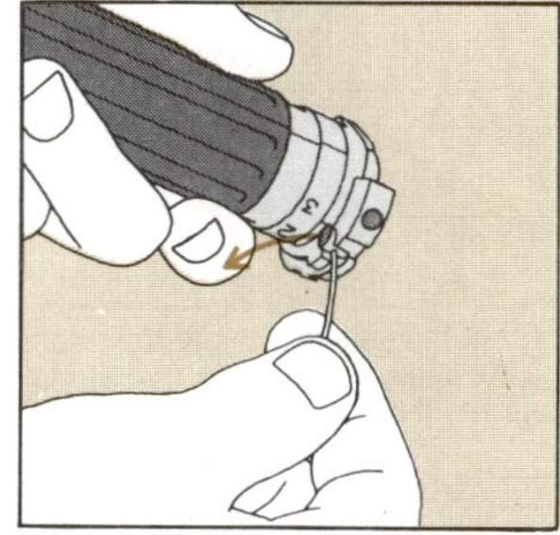

6 Remove the cable nipple from its housing. Fit the new cable and reassemble in the reverse order

Replacing a gear cable

A Derailleur gear consists of a multi-sprocket freewheel unit and a carrier mechanism to direct the chain from one sprocket to another. Gear is changed with a control lever mounted on the frame tube. The most likely faults are a broken control cable and a badly adjusted guide mechanism. A new chain has to be riveted together—a job best left to a dealer.

Materials: new inner control cable; plastic protector sleeve for the cable.
Tools: small screwdriver; pliers; spanner to fit the cable clevis nut; screwdriver for the control lever centre bolt.

1 Remove the old cable, put the gear lever in the halfway position, and insert the new cable

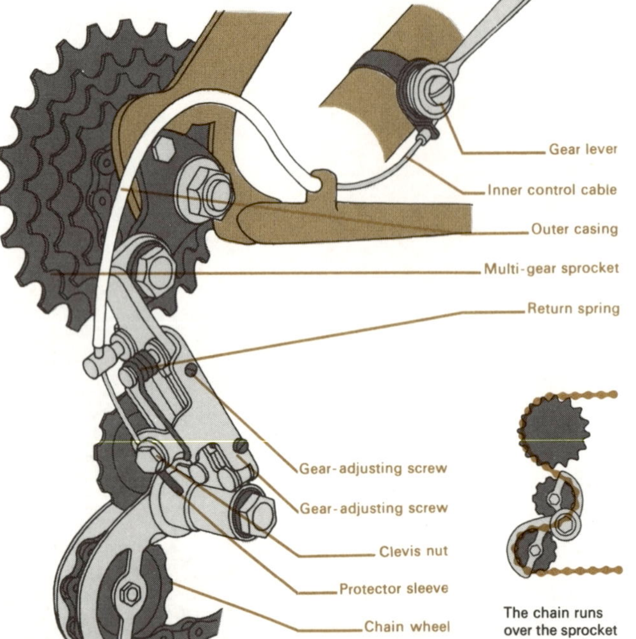

The chain runs over the sprocket and round the carrier wheels

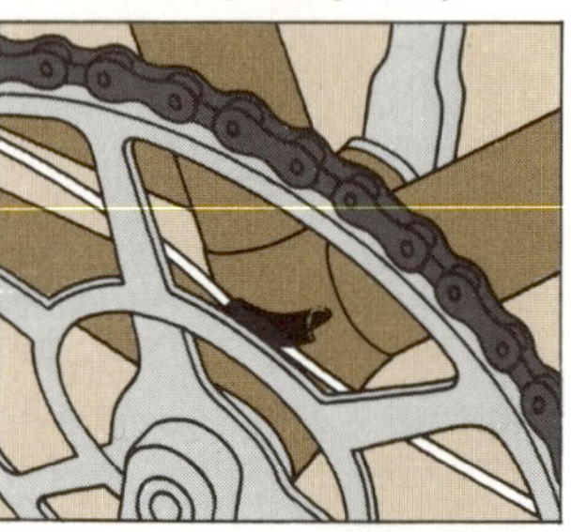

2 Pull the lever right back—this avoids kinking the cable—and feed the cable through the guide eye

3 Feed the cable through the guide channel just above the bottom bracket of the cycle frame

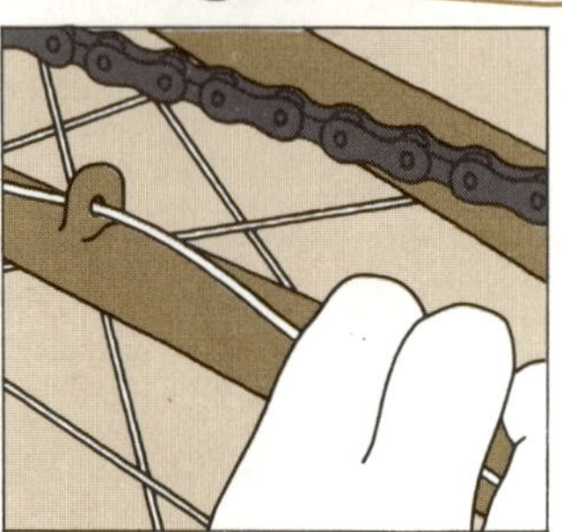

4 Slip it through the eye on the multi-gear sprocket side of the horizontal rear-fork stay

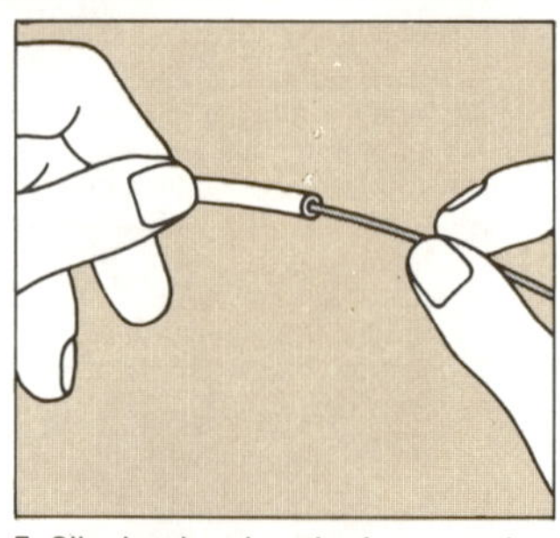

5 Slip the short length of outer casing over the cable. This casing will butt against the eye on the rear-fork stay

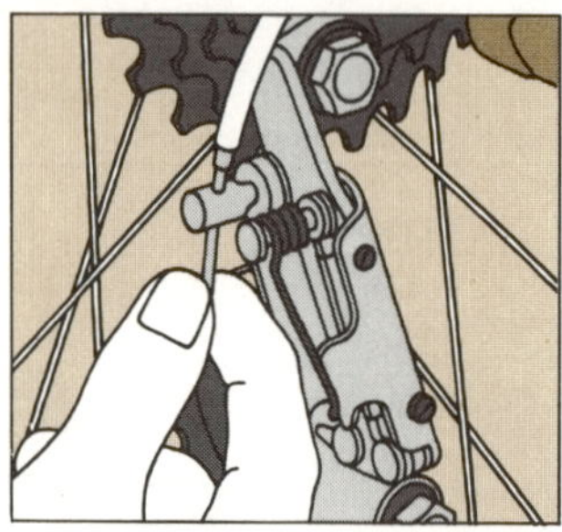

6 Slide the cable through the guide on the carrier mechanism. The casing must rest in the stop

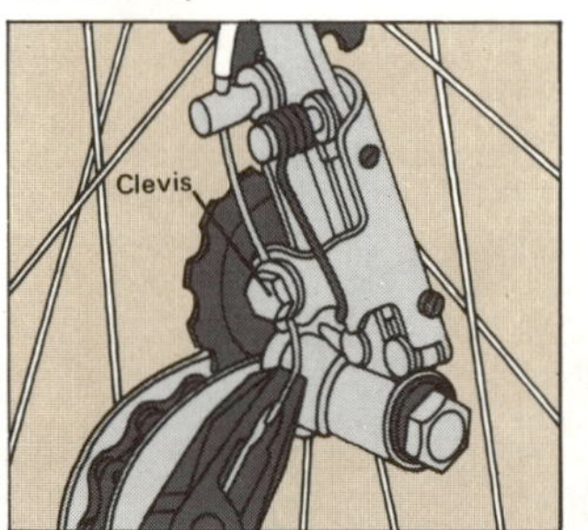

7 Put the gear lever right forward and fit the cable to the clevis. Pull tight and tighten the clevis nut (arrowed)

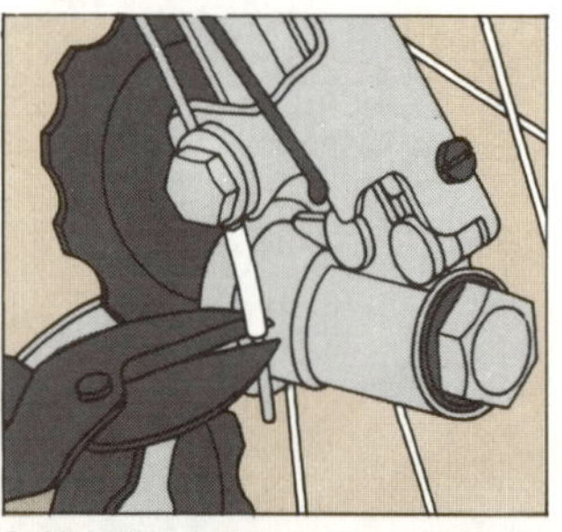

8 Slide the protector sleeve over the cable, up to the clevis, and cut off the surplus cable below it

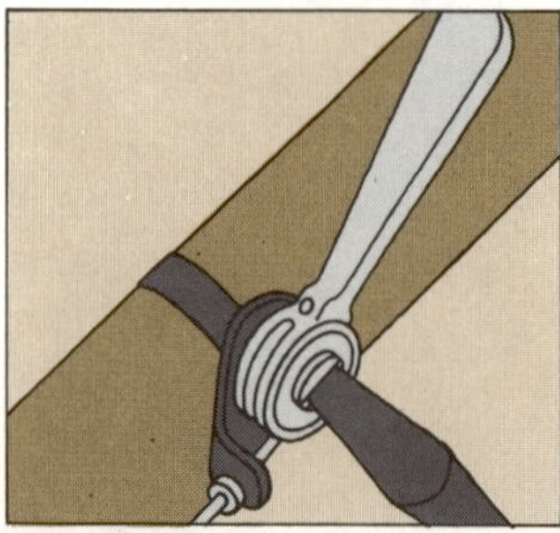

9 Check that the centre bolt on the gear lever is tight, so that the lever holds in any position

Adjusting a five-speed gear

1 Put the gear in 'bottom'; screw in the top adjuster until the chain rides centrally on the largest sprocket without slipping over (overriding) the top

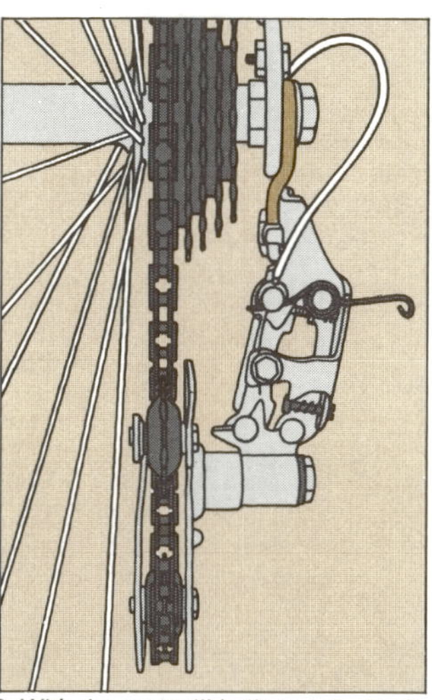

2 With the gear still in 'bottom', check the clearance between the carrier mechanism and the spokes. As little as $\frac{1}{8}$ in. (3 mm) is sufficient

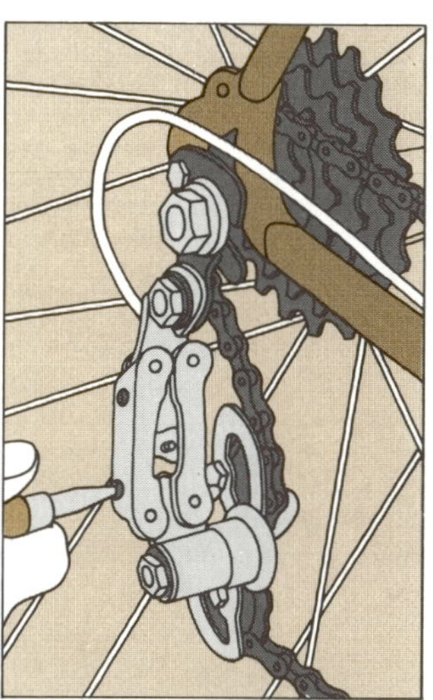

3 With the gear in 'top', screw in the bottom adjuster until the chain rides the smallest sprocket centrally, but without overriding it

Removing a Derailleur-gear rear wheel

1 Holding the wheel with one hand to prevent it moving, loosen the wheel nuts with a spanner

2 Still holding the wheel, draw the guide mechanism back against the spring pressure and hold it there

3 Move the wheel forwards and lift it off between the upper and lower parts of the chain

Adjusting a ten-speed gear

By using the normal five-sprocket rear-hub gear and a double-chain wheel on the front, ten speeds are available. Adjust the rear carrier mechanism in the same way as a five-speed gear. The chain-guide mechanism at the front must be correctly set to prevent the chain overriding when the gear selection is made.

Tools: small screwdriver; steel straight-edge.

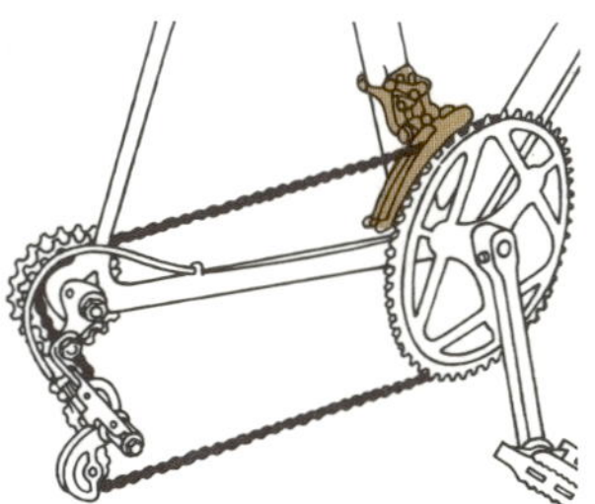

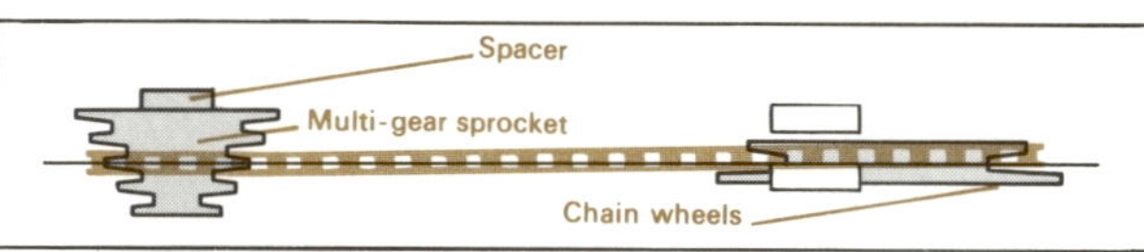

1 Check the alignment of the front and rear sprockets. The rear centre sprocket must line up centrally between the two front sprockets. If necessary, insert spacers between the hub and rear sprocket to give alignment

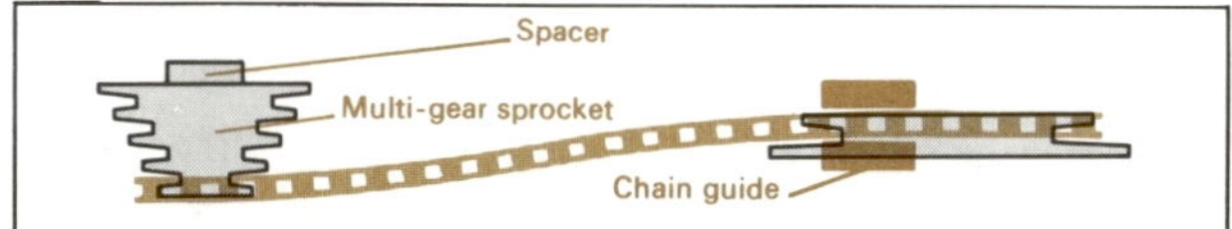

2 In this intermediate gear, with the chain riding on the rear outside sprocket and the front inside sprocket, see that the chain guide does not foul the chain while preventing it overriding the chain wheel

3 Two screws on the top of the chain-guide mechanism provide for adjustment of the guide

4 Turn each screw until the chain does not override the sprockets and is free of the guide

Freewheel sprocket

Replacing a sprocket

Though it is possible to dismantle a freewheel sprocket, spare parts are difficult to obtain. If the sprocket starts to slip—the first sign of failure—it must be replaced. The sprocket also has to be removed for replacement of a wheel spoke on the gear side of the hub. In both cases a sprocket extractor is needed; as there are patterns to suit the several different types of freewheel unit, take the wheel to the shop when buying one. If a new sprocket is needed, choose one with the same number of teeth as the sprocket being replaced.

Materials: new freewheel sprocket.
Tools: wheel-nut spanner; sprocket extractor; vice or spanner to fit extractor nut.

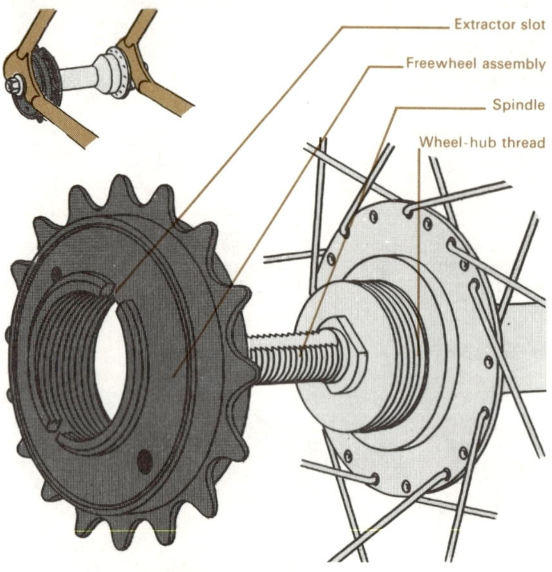

TYPES OF SPROCKET EXTRACTORS

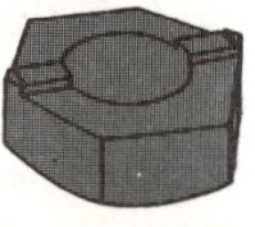

1 Take off the nuts and remove the wheel from the frame. Secure the wheel spindle in a vice, freewheel upwards

2 Place the sprocket extractor over the spindle and make sure its pegs engage in the slots of the freewheel unit

3 With the extractor in position, screw one of the wheel nuts down the spindle until it touches the extractor

4 Tighten the wheel nut with a spanner to the same tightness as is needed to hold the wheel in the cycle frame

5 Take the wheel from the vice, turn it over, then tighten the jaws of the vice on to the extractor tool

6 Grip the wheel rim and turn the wheel anti-clockwise just enough to loosen the gear unit on the wheel-hub thread

7 Remove the wheel, turn it over and grip the spindle in the vice. Undo the wheel nut above the extractor

Freewheel sprocket

8 With the nut removed, use the extractor to unscrew the freewheel unit so that it can be lifted off the hub

9 Fit the new freewheel sprocket and tighten it by hand. The normal action of pedalling will tighten it fully

Five-speed sprocket

Removing and replacing a five-speed sprocket

Always use an extractor tool to remove a five-speed sprocket for cleaning or replacement. After replacing the sprocket, you may find that the gears will start to slip. This is because the sprocket, the chain and the chain wheel no longer fit together due to wear. In this case, a new chain and chain wheel may have to be fitted.

Make sure you do not cross-thread the freewheel, as this could damage the thread on the freewheel and on the wheel itself. Always clean the dirt from the thread of the hub.

Materials: five-speed sprocket.
Tools: vice; sprocket extractor.

Loosening a sprocket In order to loosen and then remove a sprocket, it is necessary to use a work-bench vice.

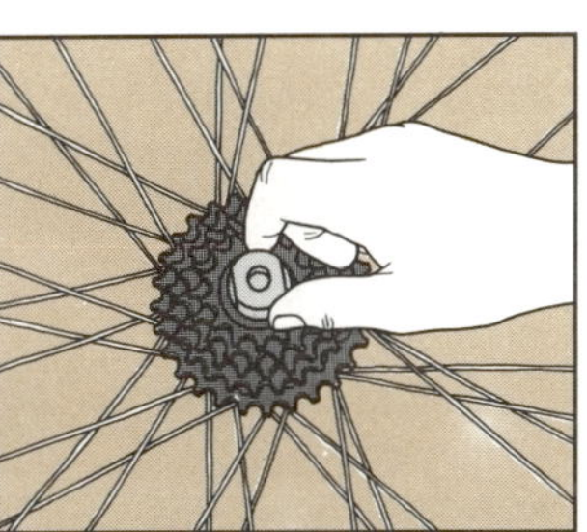

1 Place the sprocket extractor over the spindle until it engages into the sprocket pegs. Replace a nut over the extractor and tighten

2 Place the sprocket extractor into the jaws of a vice and tighten. Turn the wheel anti-clockwise until the sprocket gives (see left)

3 Remove the nut from the spindle, then remove the sprocket by hand. Replace the new sprocket and tighten it by hand

Brakes

Blocks

Adjusting brakes and fitting new blocks

The cable brakes shown are the ones most commonly used today. Other kinds work on the same principle—a split caliper is operated by an inner and outer cable. Adjustment, and the fitting of new blocks, is the same for all types; but choose new blocks that will fit the shoes. Adjust brakes so that the blocks are about $\frac{1}{8}$ in. (3 mm) from the rim. To draw the shoes closer to the wheel, turn the knurled adjuster anti-clockwise.

Materials: a set of brake blocks.
Tools: spanner to fit brake shoe nut.

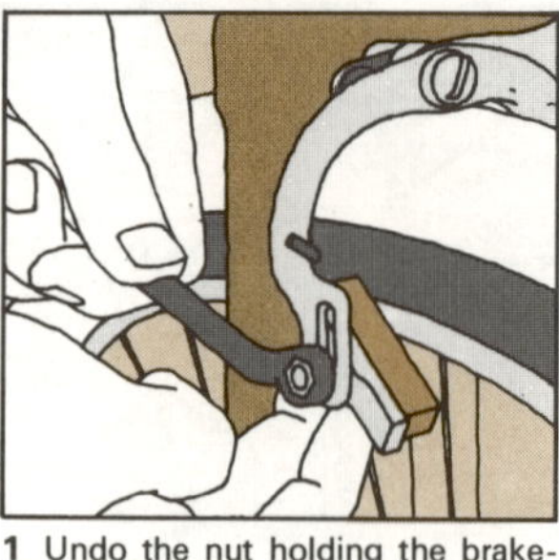

1 Undo the nut holding the brake-block shoe to the caliper base and slide out the shoe assembly

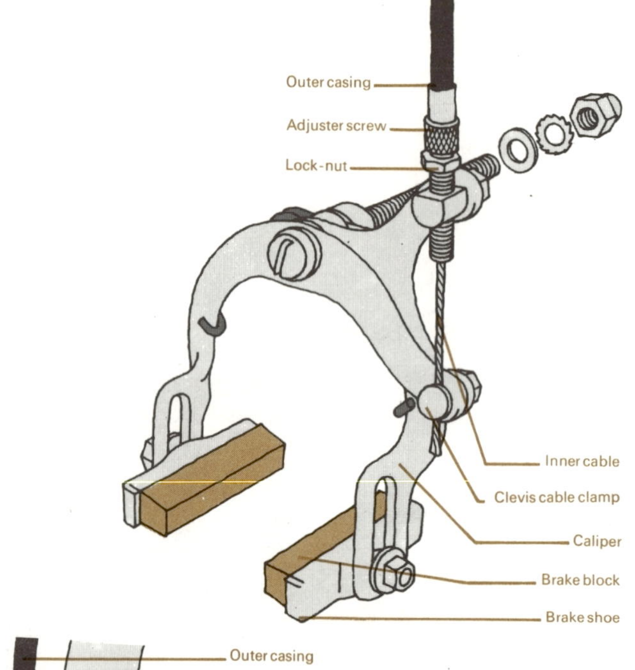

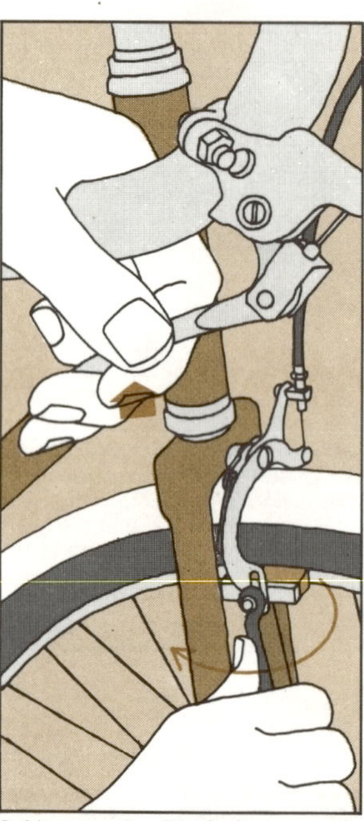

2 Line up the fitted shoes evenly with the rim and hold them firm *with the brake on* when tightening up

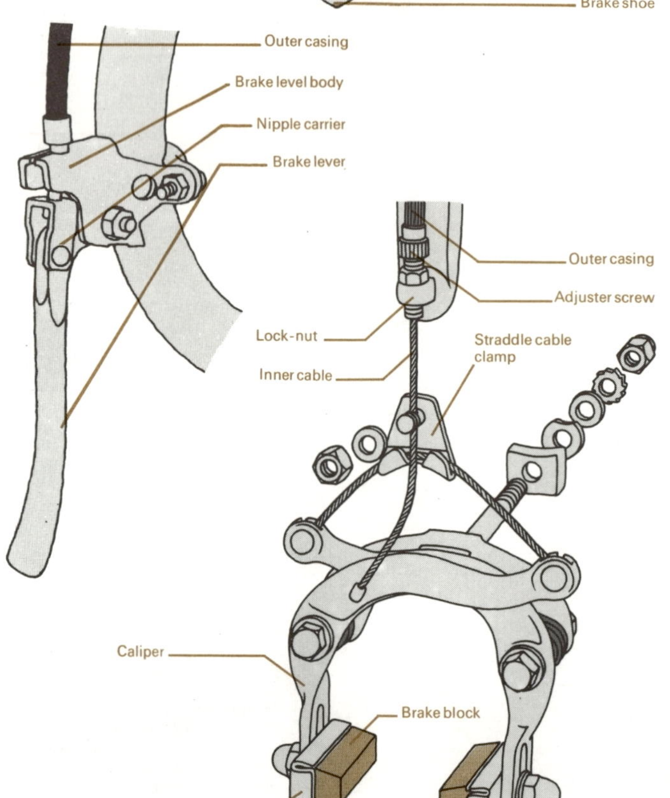

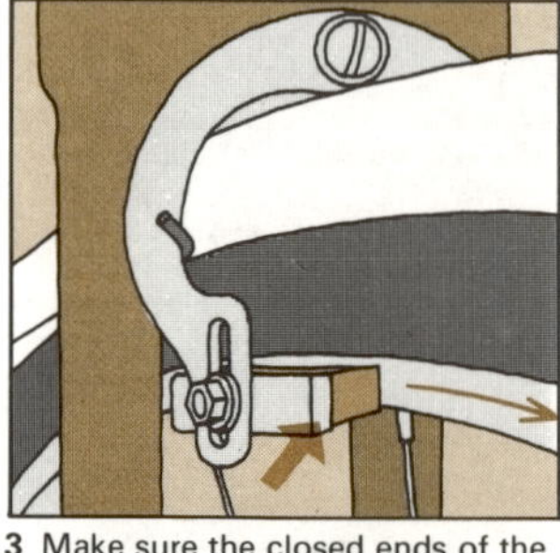

3 Make sure the closed ends of the shoes face in the same direction as the rotation of the wheel

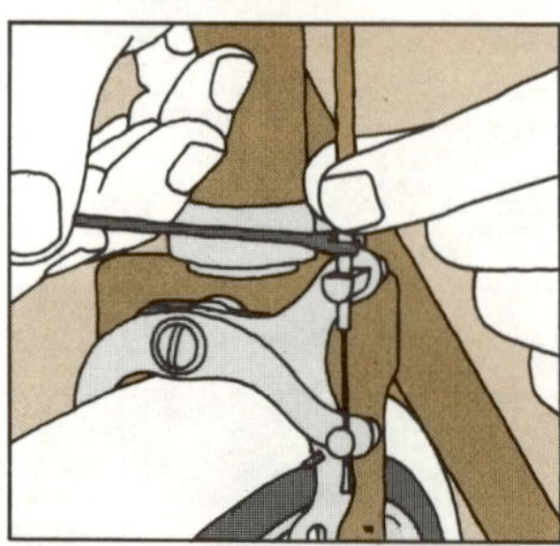

4 Turn the adjuster screw to get the correct brake position. Lock the screw with the lock-nut

Replacing and adjusting brake cables

When a brake cable breaks it must be replaced *immediately,* as a cyclist is legally required to have fully operative front and rear brakes. There are two types of brake cable: centre-pull and side-pull. The stronger centre-pull cables are fitted on to racing cycles; all other types of cycle have side-pull brakes. There are two main types of cables—those with barrel-shaped nipples and those with pear-shaped. Either type can be used on side-pull or centre-pull units.

Front and rear brake cables should be regularly checked to make sure that the inner cables are not frayed and that the outer casings are not stretched. Regular lubrication gives the cables and the casings a longer and more efficient working life.

All cable-operated brake units have a nut to adjust the tension and to keep the brakes as close as is practical to the rims of the bicycle wheels.

There are six stages in replacing either type of brake cable—the first four of which are the same in both cases. But the last two stages are different—as shown in the diagrams below.

When the cable has been replaced, press the brake lever two or three times so that everything 'draws together'. If the brake cable is slack at the bottom, turn the adjuster screw in an anti-clockwise direction until the cable is firmly located.

Materials: new brake cable; new outer casing if necessary; lubricating oil.
Tools: small spanner; pair of flat pliers.

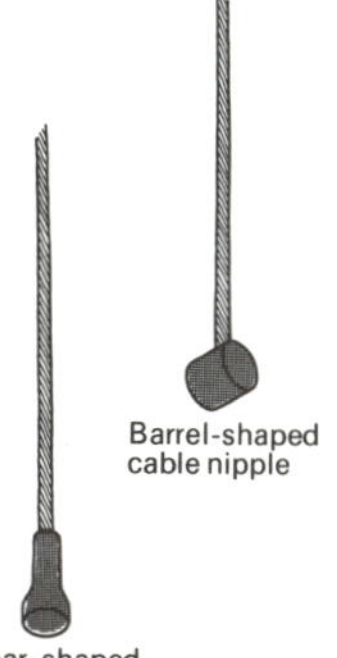

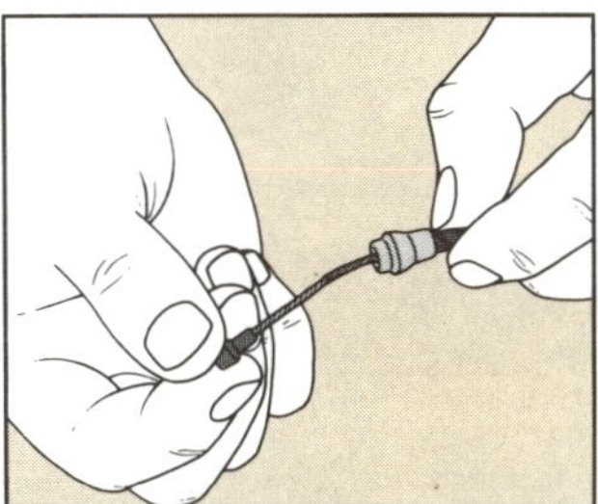

1 Remove the old cable from its outer casing. Keep the ferrule for use with the new cable

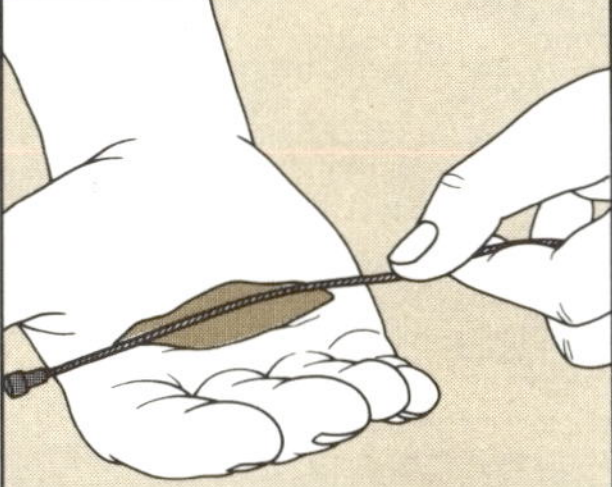

2 Put a little oil in the palm of your hand ready to lubricate the new cable as it is threaded through the ferrule

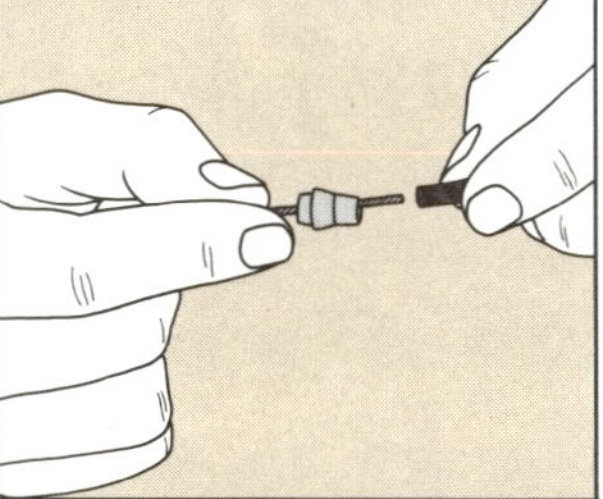

3 Thread the new cable through the ferrule and then into the cable outer casing

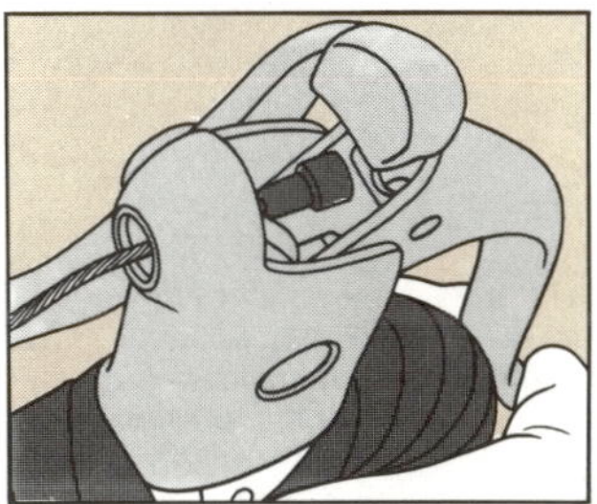

4 Pull the brake lever towards the handlebars and fit the cable nipple into the nipple holder

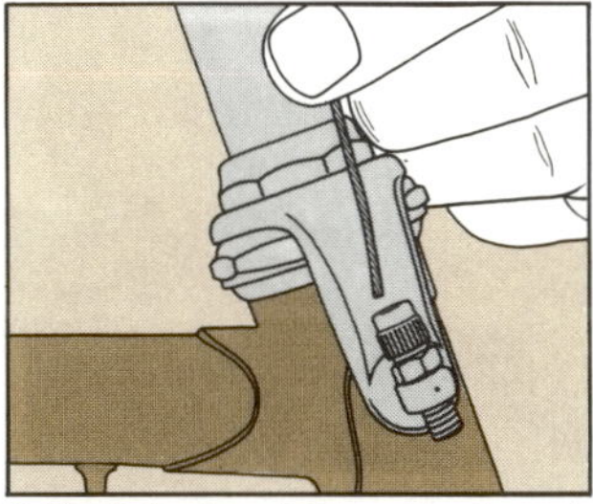

5 Carefully thread the cable through the adjuster and then through the triangular-shaped straddle

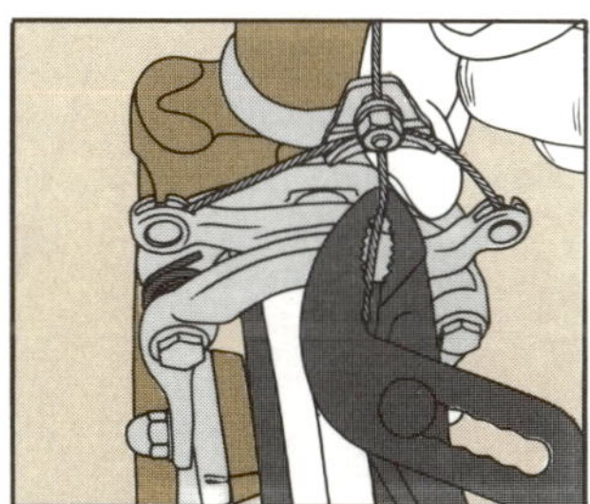

6 Connect straddle to straddle cable. Pull cable through with pliers and tighten with a spanner

SIDE-PULL BRAKE CABLE ALTERNATIVE STAGES

For bicycles fitted with a side-pull cable, complete the first four stages as shown in the above illustrations. Then complete the last two stages as shown in the illustrations on the right.

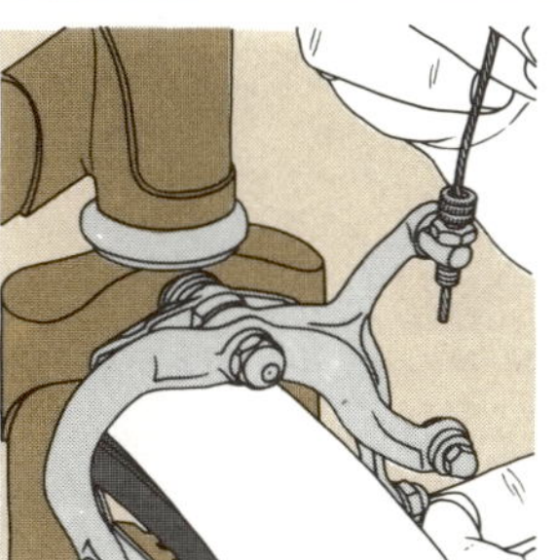

5 Carefully thread the cable through the adjuster by hand, and then thread it through the clevis clamp bolt

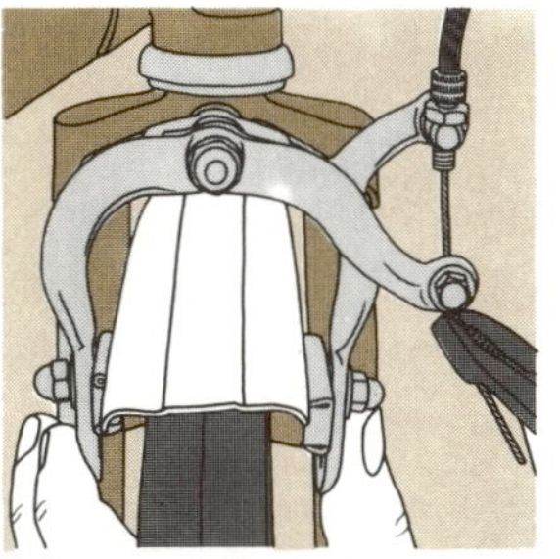

6 Squeeze the brake blocks on to the rims and pull cable through with pliers. Then tighten the clevis clamp bolt

Brake adjustment

Before adjusting the brakes, check that the pivot points on the rod linkage are lubricated and move freely. Straighten any bent rods. Fit new blocks by the method given for cable brakes on p. 22.

Tools: spanners to fit lock-nut on rear stirrup and clevis nuts; screwdriver.

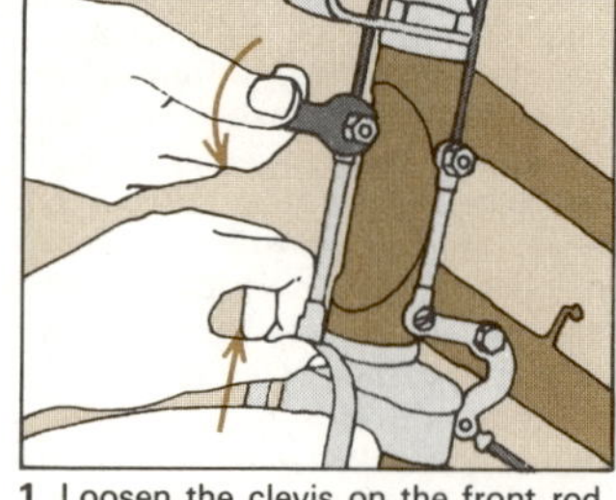

1 Loosen the clevis on the front rod. Holding the lever down, lift the stirrup so that the brake rod slides further down into the tube

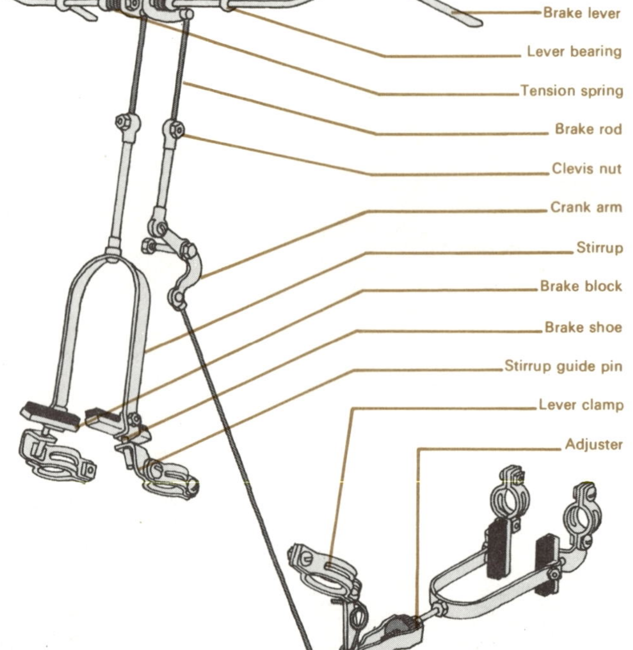

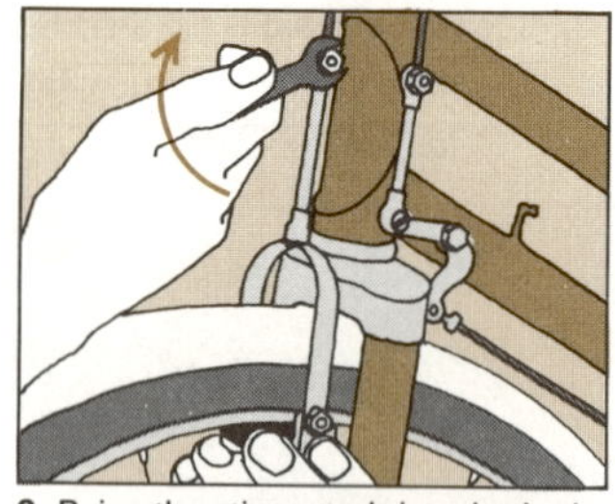

2 Raise the stirrup to bring the brake blocks about $\frac{1}{8}$ in. (3 mm) clear of the rim of the wheel. Tighten the clevis nut to secure

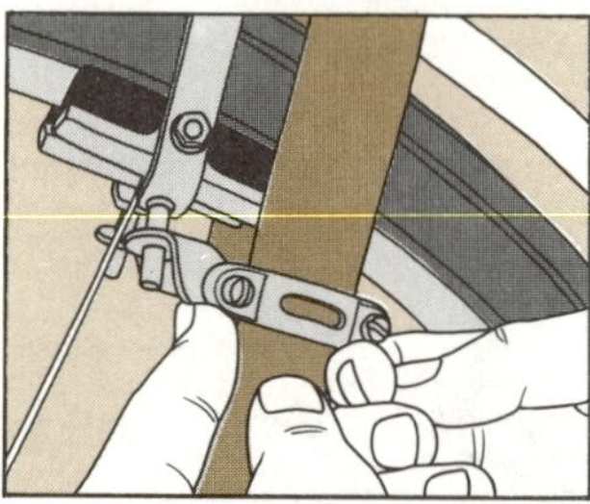

3 Move the stirrup guides up the fork legs, so that the stirrup pins do not come out when the brakes are applied

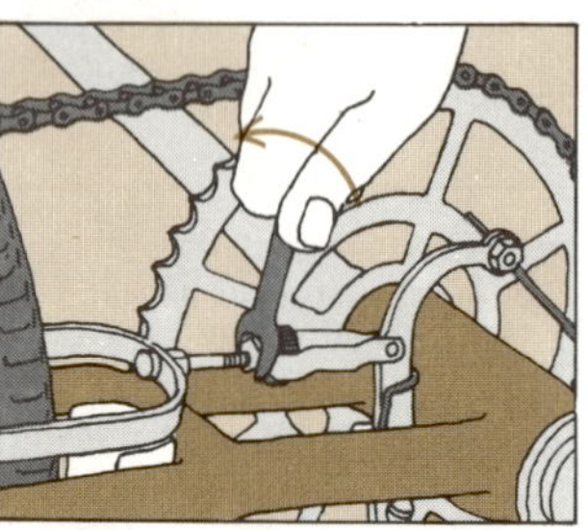

4 Turn the cycle upside-down, loosen the lock-nut on the adjuster with a spanner, and run the nut to the end of the thread

5 Move the stirrup until the blocks are about $\frac{1}{8}$ in. (3 mm) from the rim. Screw the adjuster to secure it, then tighten the lock-nut

6 Check the tightness of the clevis that secures the down-tube brake rod to the stirrup. It should not require any adjustment

7 After brake adjustment, the stirrup guides may also need adjusting. The first step is to loosen the screws on the clamp

8 Tap the guides along the frame tubes, with the stirrup pins in the guide holes, until the guides are about $\frac{1}{4}$ in. (6 mm) away from the stirrup

9 If the rear brake is similar to the front brake, adjust it by loosening the nut and sliding the stirrup along the brake rod

Fitting new front shoes

Brake shoes on a hub-brake assembly need replacing if they are worn down to the rivets or have become oily from a leak in the bearings. In the latter case, a new bearing sealing-ring must be fitted. It is not worth spending time re-lining the shoes; instead, buy replacement shoes or, for rear wheels, a complete new assembly. To fit new shoes the wheel must be removed and the hub brake stripped down. A new assembly is needed for rear wheels because the smaller size of the drum makes it impracticable to fit replacement shoes.

Materials: front-brake replacement shoes, or a complete brake assembly for rear hub; grease.
Tools: spanners to fit hub wheel-nuts, brake-arm nut and shoe pivot bolt; screwdriver.

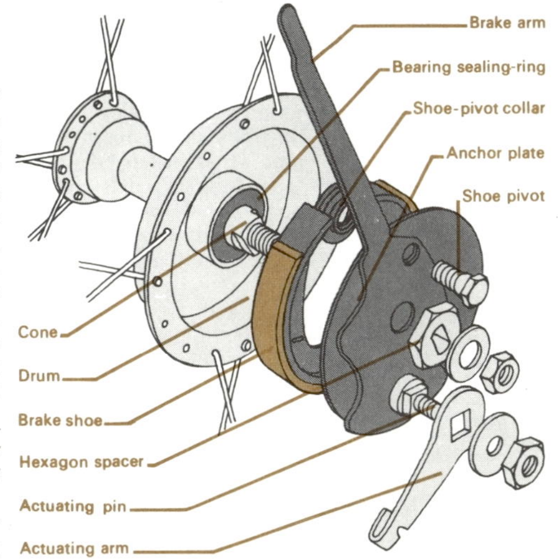

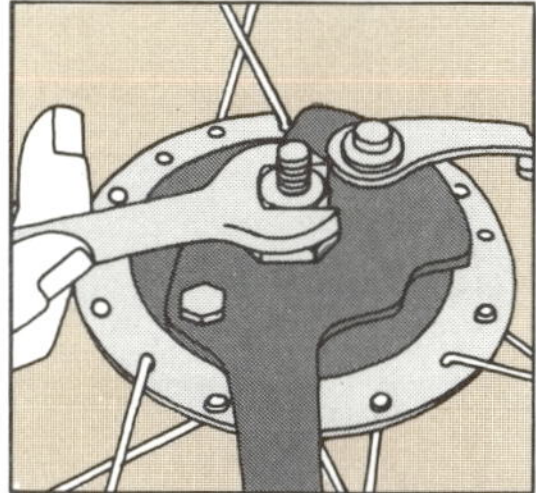

1 Take off the front wheel and hold the spindle in a vice, brake drum uppermost. Remove the lock-nut and washer

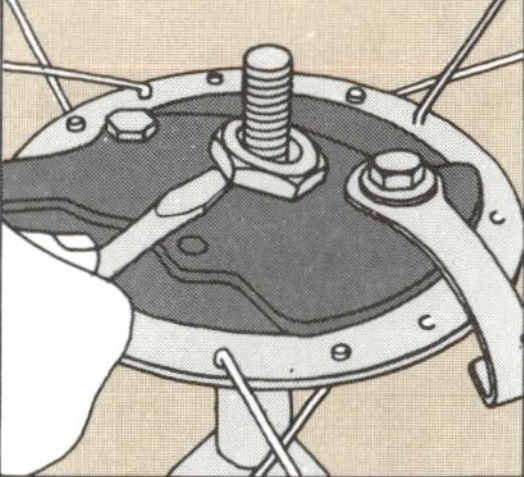

2 Prise the hexagon spacer off the shaft with a screwdriver. The spacer fits over the flattened edges of the cone

3 Hold the anchor plate by either the brake arm or the actuating arm and lift up to remove the complete assembly

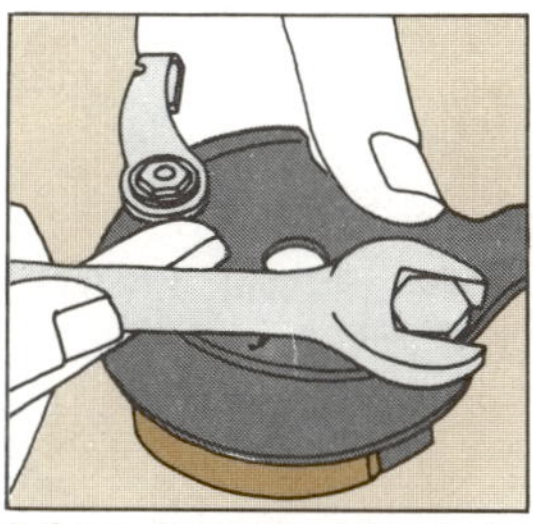

4 Start dismantling the brake shoes by undoing the bolt holding the shoe pivot. This is on the outside of the brake plate

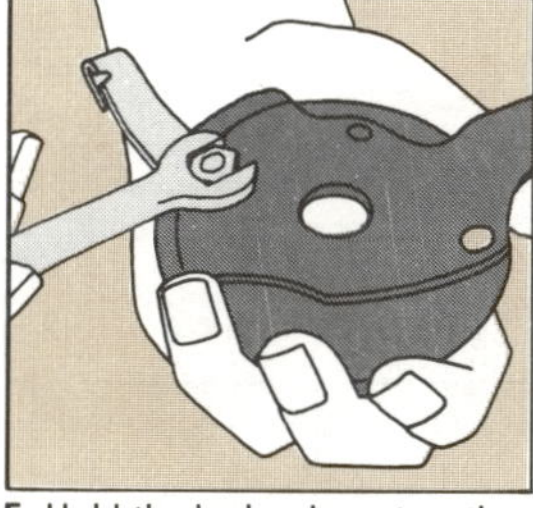

5 Hold the brake shoes together in one hand to prevent them opening, and undo the nut securing the actuating arm

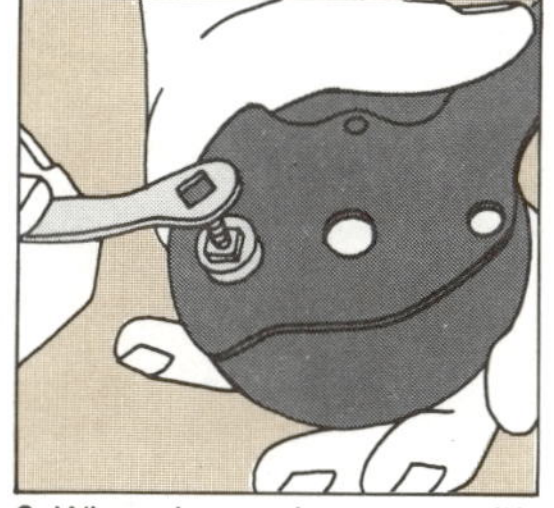

6 When the nut is removed, lift off the actuating arm. It fits over a squared spindle, so note how it is positioned

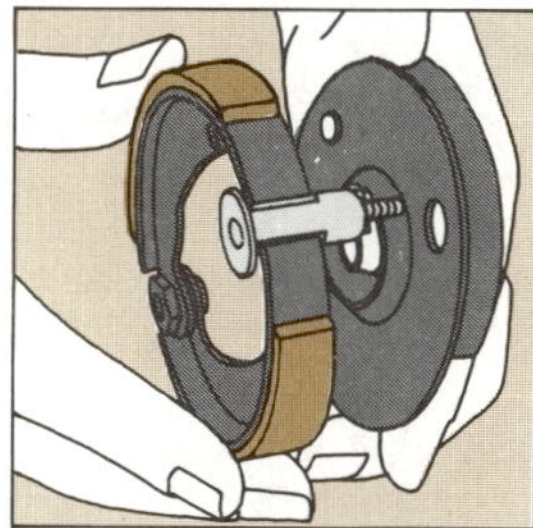

7 Now draw away the complete brake-shoe assembly, together with the actuating pin, from the anchor plate

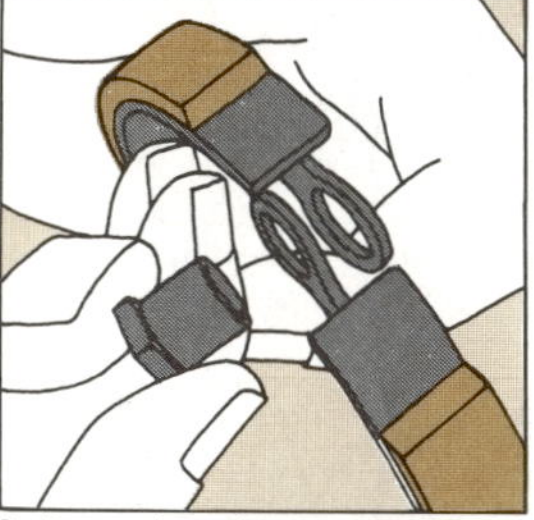

8 Press the shoes together to remove the pivot collar from the shoe eyes. Renew the collar if it is showing signs of wear

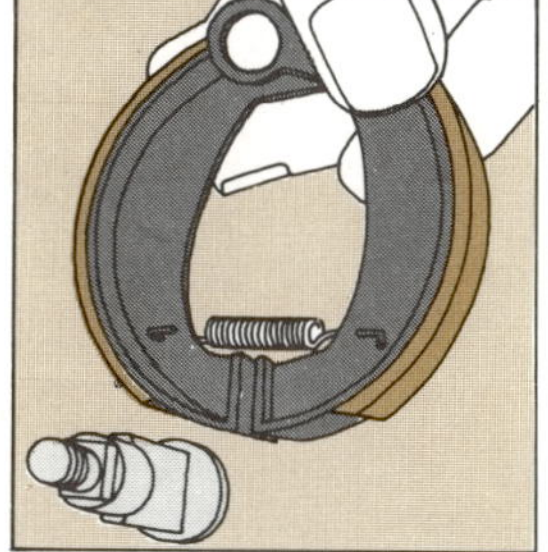

9 Overlap the eyes, spreading the lower end against the spring pressure. Remove the pin

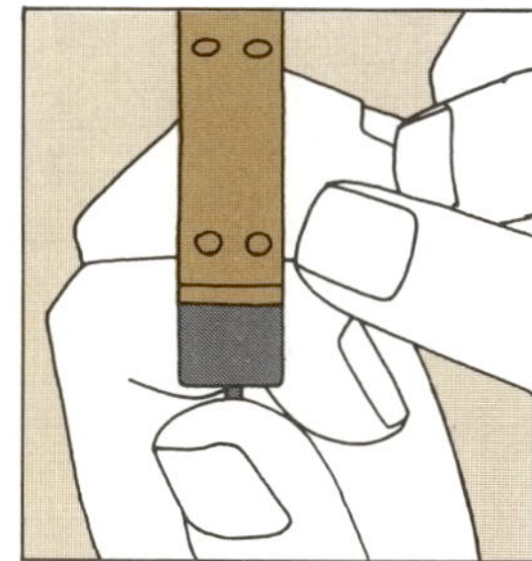

10 Fit new brake-shoe linings if they are dirty from oil or worn down to the rivets

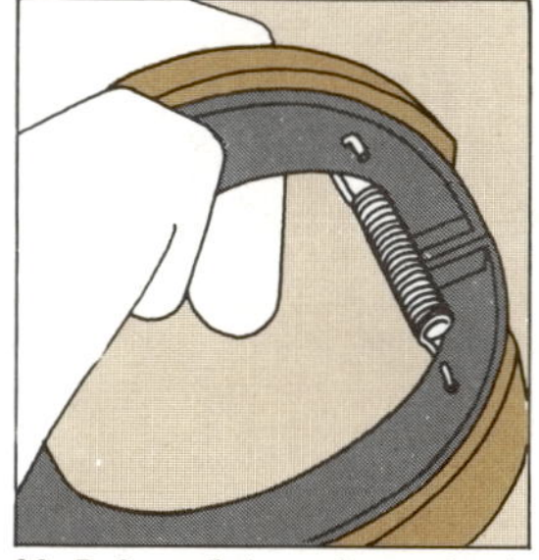

11 Before fitting shoes, hook the return spring into the shoe holes to bring the shoes together

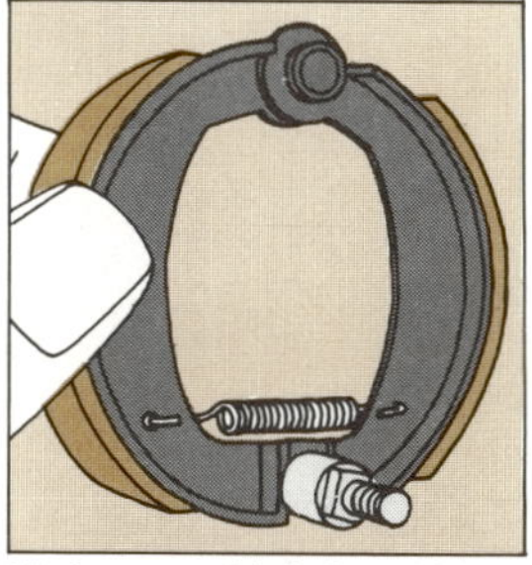

12 A reassembled shoe. Lightly grease the actuating pin and pivot collar before replacing

Coaster hubs

Renewing the bearings

Coaster hubs—or back-pedalling brake hubs as they are more commonly called—seldom give trouble. The freewheel mechanism inside the hub is sturdily made, but the bearings and cones may occasionally need replacing. This is a fairly easy job once the hub has been stripped. The main difference between coaster-hub bearings and conventional bearings is that the ball bearings of the former are caged while those in conventional bearings are loose. Two of the most popular and reliable coaster brakes are the Shimano 3SC and the Sturmey-Archer S3C.

Materials: new ball-bearing cages; bearing cones; new brake mechanism if the present one is worn.

Tools: hammer, punch; C spanner for lock-ring; screwdriver; hardwood block.

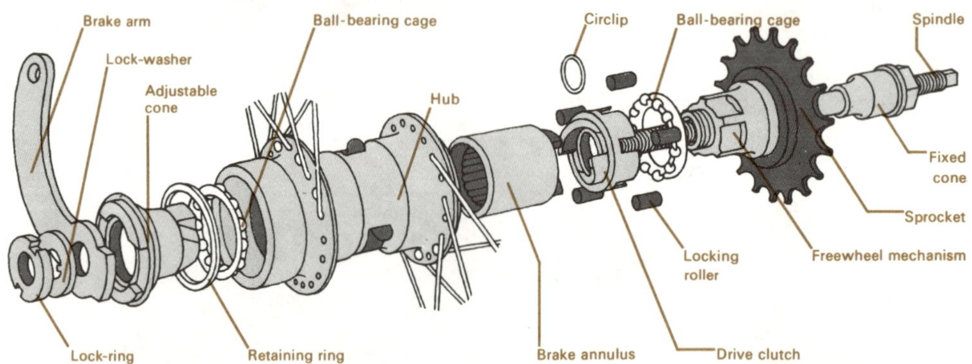

BRAKE-ARM CLIP

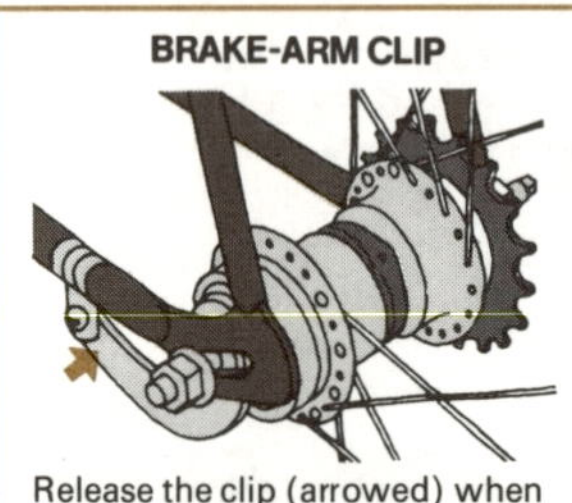

Release the clip (arrowed) when removing the wheel. When replacing, make sure to tighten the clip securely

1 Use a C spanner, or a hammer and punch, to loosen and remove the lock-ring from the shaft

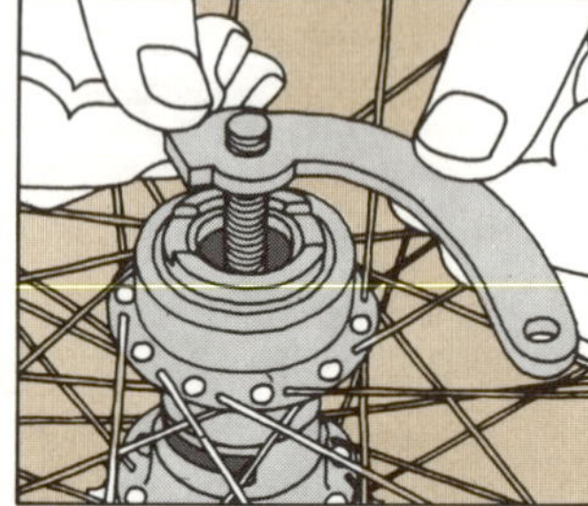

2 Remove the brake arm from the slots in the adjustable cone head, tapping the arm free if it is tight

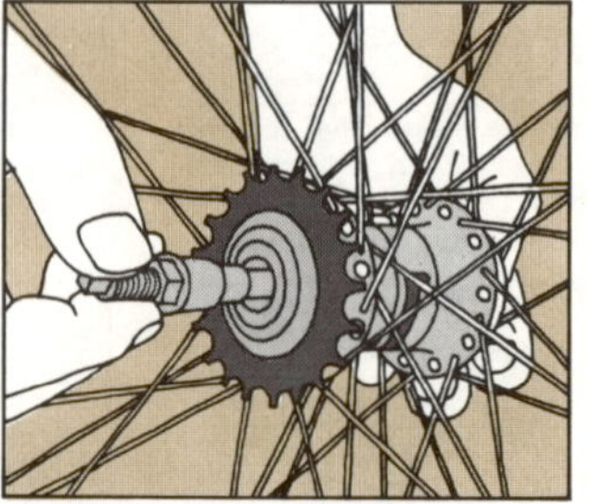

3 Hold the adjustable cone firm and unscrew the spindle, drawing it out of the hub as you unscrew it

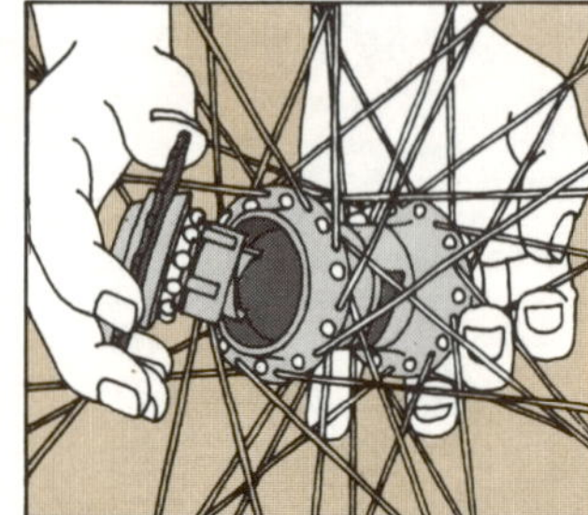

4 With the spindle removed, lift the sprocket and freewheel mechanism from the hub as a single unit

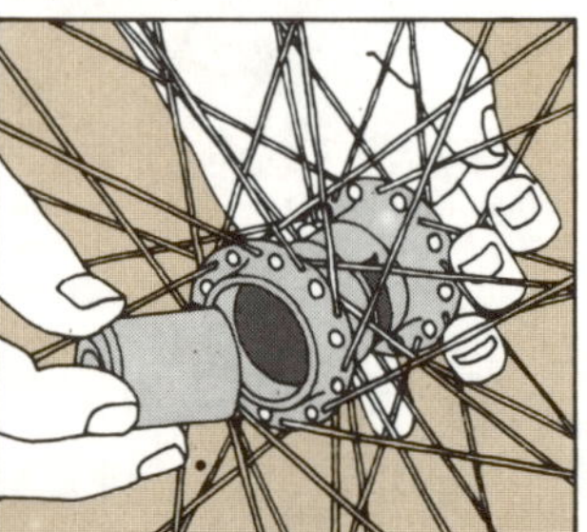

5 Tilt the open end of the hub towards your hand and collect the brake annulus and lock mechanism

6 Tilt the hub the opposite way and empty out the adjustable cone from the other end of the hub

Coaster hubs

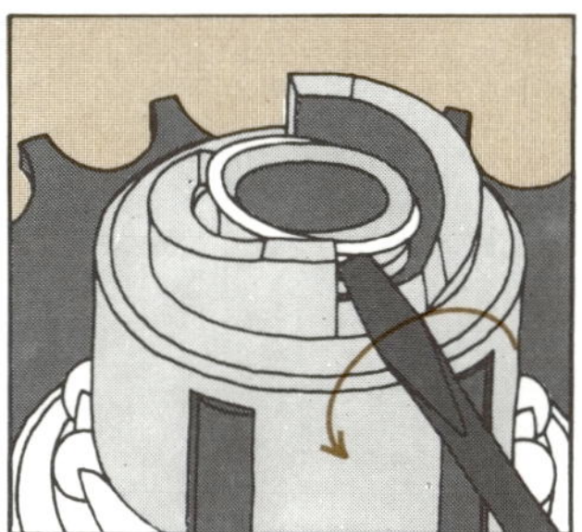
7 To start renewing bearings on the freewheel side, lift the circlip off the drive clutch with a screwdriver

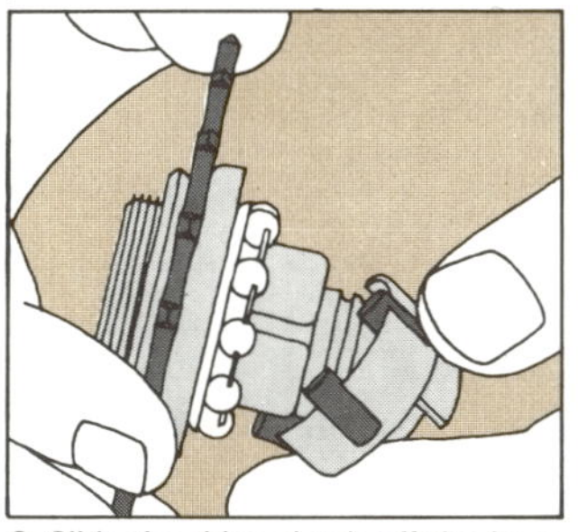
8 Slide the drive clutch off the boss, taking care not to lose any of the five locking rollers that may drop out

9 Lift the ball cage, which is part of the freewheel mechanism, off the cone. Check the cone for wear

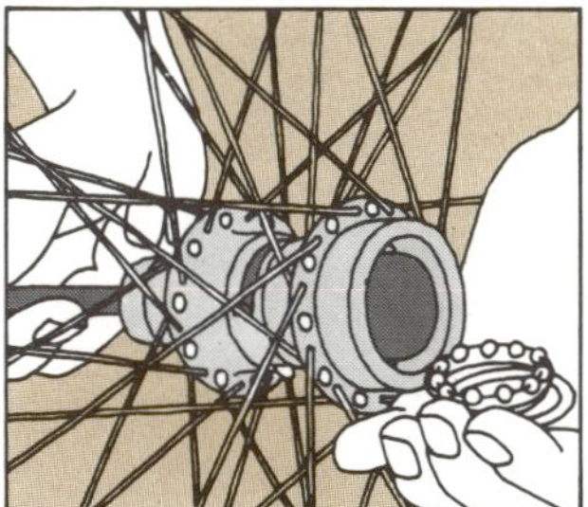
10 With a screwdriver handle, tap out the other ball cage and retaining ring from inside the hub

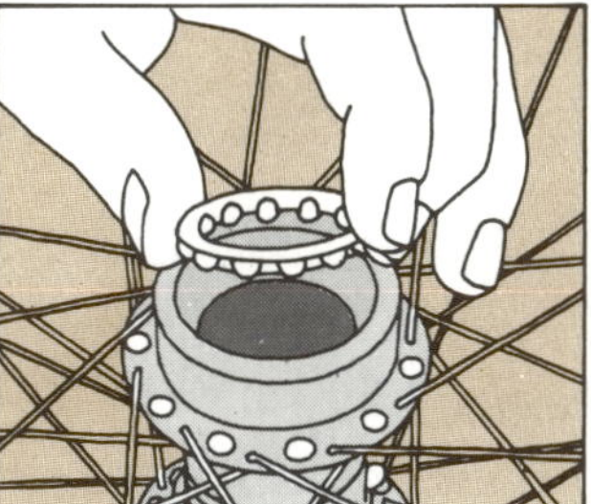
11 Clean and grease the hub-bearing cup and fit the new ball cage with the ball bearings towards the cup

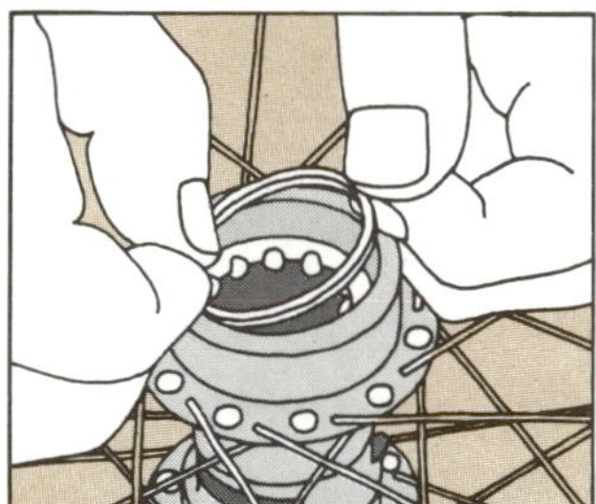
12 Fit a new retaining ring, recessed side away from the cage. Tap in with a hammer and hardwood block

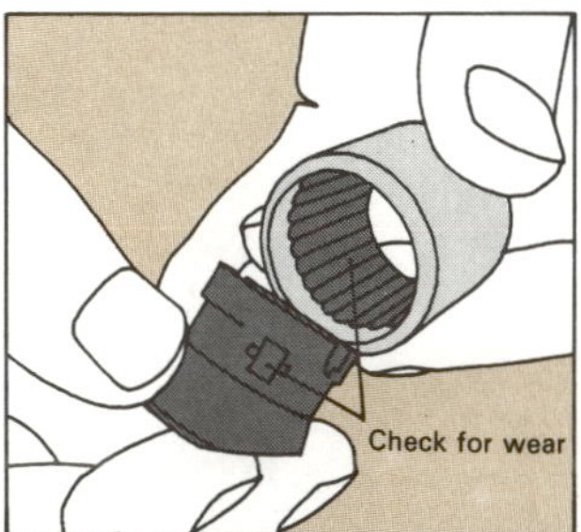

13 If the brake annulus grooves or lock mechanism are worn, refit a complete new brake mechanism

14 Grease the freewheel-mechanism cone and roller slots. Fit a new ball cage and refit the rollers

15 Slide the drive clutch over the freewheel-mechanism boss, each slot locating over a roller

16 Place the sprocket face down. Tap the circlip into its groove with a hammer and tube

17 Refit the mechanism to the hub so that the clutch driving dogs engage with those on the annulus

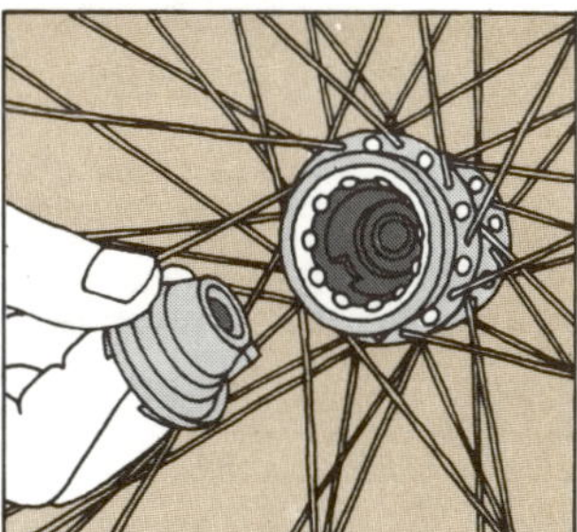
18 Refit the adjustable cone, its key in the annulus keyway. Screw in the spindle and adjust the bearings

Movable parts

Handlebars

Adjusting handlebars

Handlebars should be adjusted to the individual requirements of the rider. They must never be raised above the limit mark. There are three types of handlebar adjuster.

With the first type, unscrew the expander bolt in the centre of the handlebars about three or four turns. Tap the head of the bolt with a hammer to release the nut inside. The handlebars should then move freely and can be pulled up or pushed down. After adjustment, tighten the bolt.

With the second type, unscrew the quick-release lever two or three turns. Adjust the handlebars as required and turn the lever clockwise to tighten.

With the third type, pull the quick-release lever away from the tube and adjust the handlebars. If necessary, adjust the clamp nut slightly to return lever to fully closed position.

Materials: expander bolt; quick-release levers.
Tools: spanner; hammer.

Type 1
1 Unscrew the expander bolt and tap it down. Adjust the handlebars and fully tighten the expander bolt

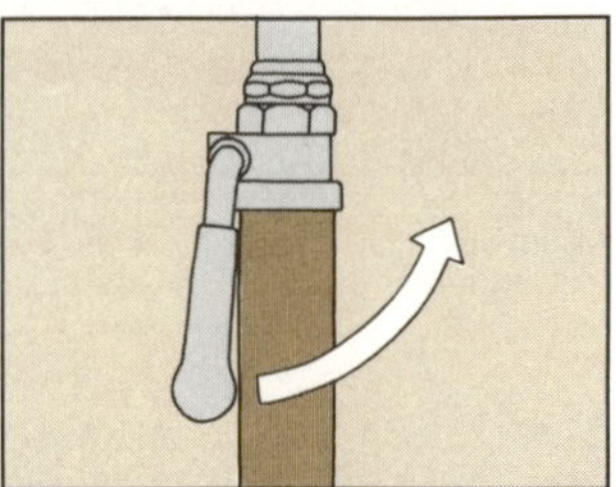

Type 2
1 Unscrew quick-release lever and then adjust handlebars. Make sure lever is returned to 'down' position

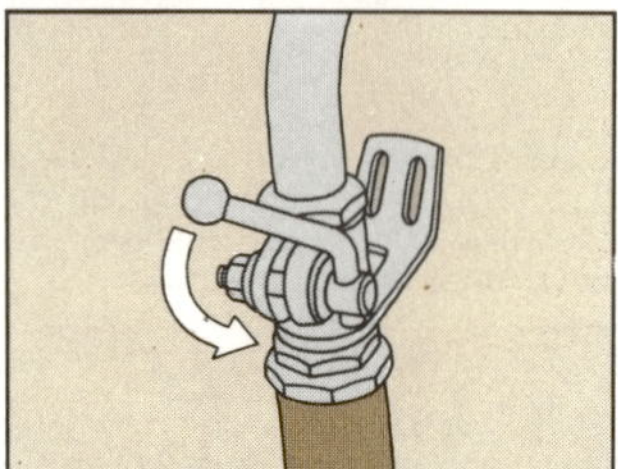

Type 3
1 Pull quick-release lever away from tube and adjust handlebars. Return lever to closed position

Steering head

Adjusting the steering head

If your cycle judders when you apply the front brake, it means that the steering-head bearings are loose. The handlebars will have too much free play and this will make steering erratic.

Loosen the locking-ring on the stem with a C spanner and push the ring up to the handlebars. If there is a lamp bracket, move it up also. Next, fully tighten the adjuster by hand. Finally, replace the locking-ring and lamp bracket and tighten fully.

If the steering head is still loose, the cups and bearings need to be replaced immediately (see p. 30).

1 Loosen the locking-ring with a C spanner or hexagonal nut spanner. Push the ring up to the handlebars by hand

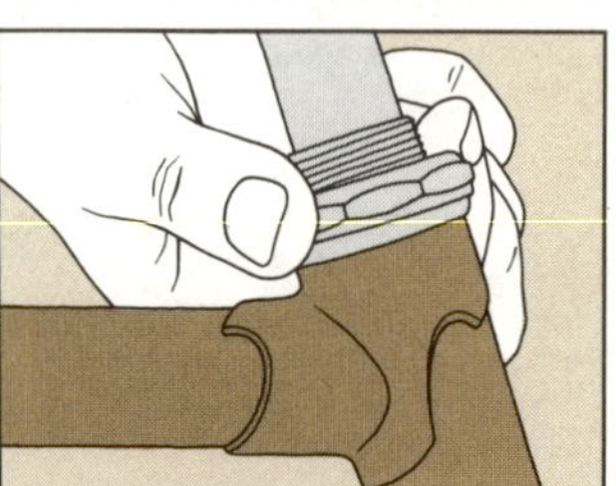

2 Fully tighten the adjuster by hand. Examine the unit to make sure there is no more free play around the top and bottom cups

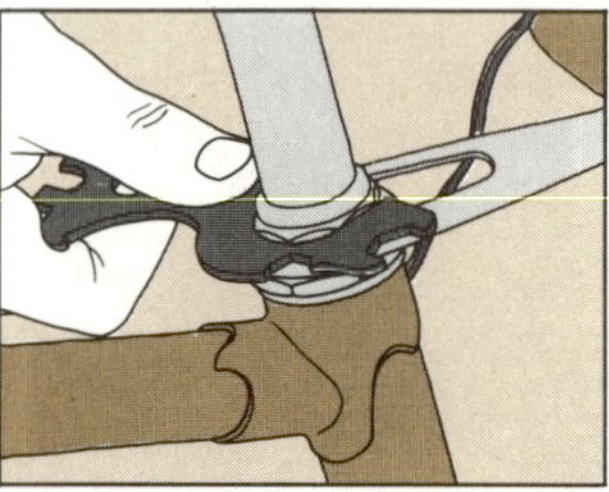

3 Replace the locking-ring and tighten fully by hand. If there is free play, cups and bearings should be replaced. Then tighten fully

Saddle

Adjusting a saddle

The saddle on a bicycle should be adjusted to suit its owner's requirements. However, it should be set so that the knee is slightly bent when the ball of the foot is on the pedal at its lowest position.

To move the saddle higher or lower, loosen the seat-tube clamp nut. Do not raise the saddle above the limit mark shown on the tube.

On most cycles the angle of the saddle can be adjusted by loosening the saddle clip and tilting the saddle either up or down. Be sure to tighten the clip again after adjustment.

1 Undo the clamp nut to move the saddle higher or lower. Do not go above the limit mark on the tube

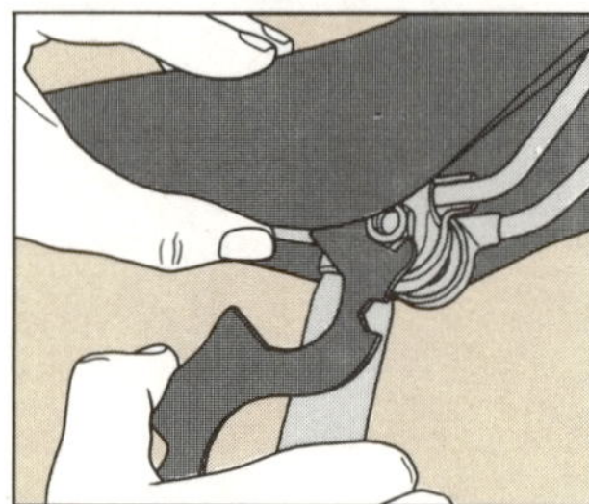

2 Loosen the saddle clip to alter the angle of the saddle. Do not fail to tighten clip afterwards

Folding mechanisms

Using folding mechanisms

Most of today's small-wheel cycles have a folding mechanism, whereby the cycle can be folded and easily carried or stored away.

The more expensive models have a locking lever which simply needs to be turned anti-clockwise to open it, allowing the cycle to be folded. Cheaper models have a locking-pin and knurled nut which, when turned and loosened, allow the locking-pin to be swung away from the tube.

Both mechanisms are tightened by working the components in a clockwise direction. In their fully closed positions, the locking levers should be parallel to the tube and point forwards.

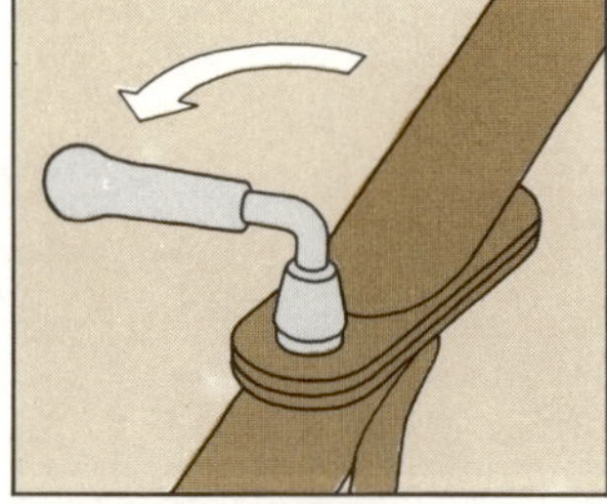

Type 1
1 Turn the locking lever in an anti-clockwise direction until it is slack. Then fold up the cycle

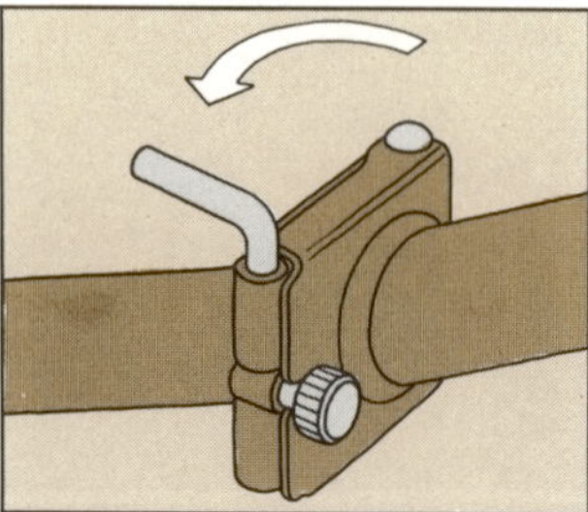

Type 2
2 Turn locking lever in an anti-clockwise direction. Then loosen knurled nut and fold up the cycle

Tapes

Replacing a tape

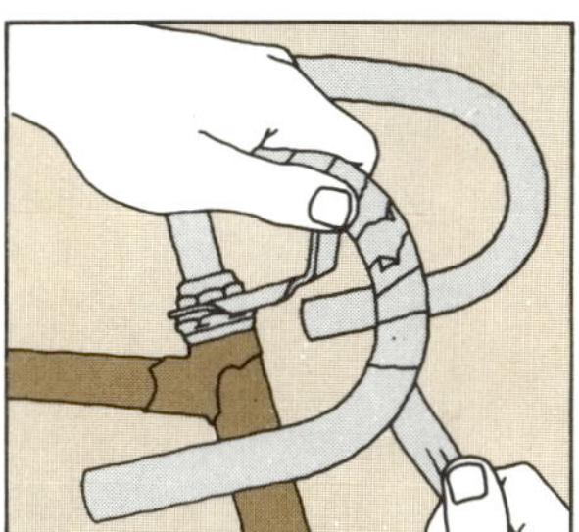

1 Remove attachments such as brake levers from the handlebars and peel off the old tape

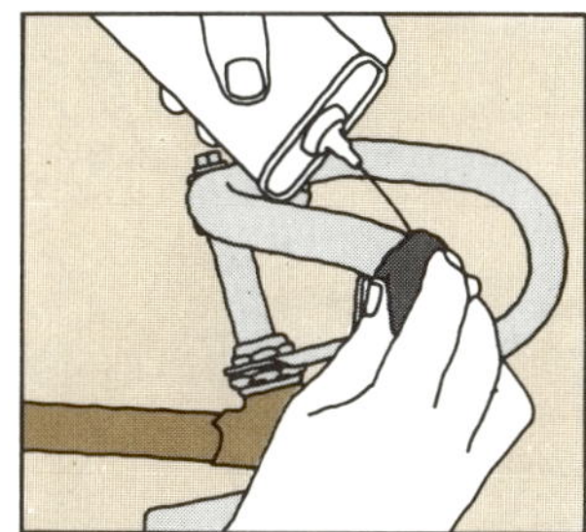

2 Clean dirt and any old adhesive off the handlebars. Petrol is an effective cleaning fluid

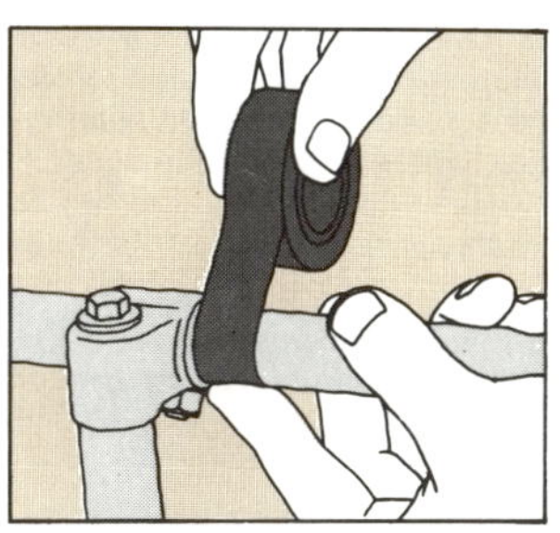

3 Start retaping at the centre of the handlebars—square at first, then at a slight angle to the bar

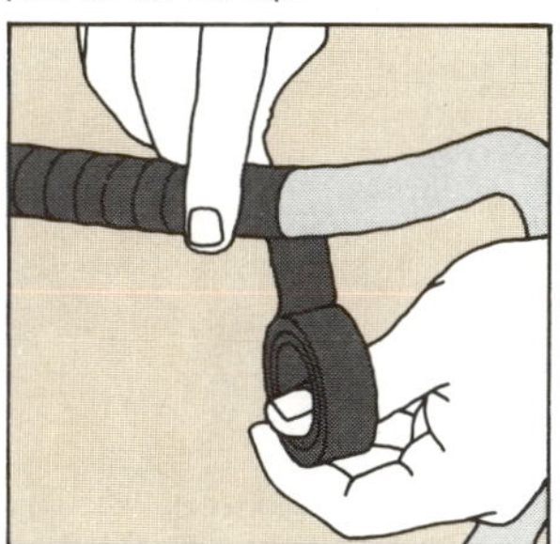

4 Press the tape into place as it is wound. Half cover each coil to get a flat even surface

5 Avoid creases and ridged edges when winding round curves, if necessary stretching the tape

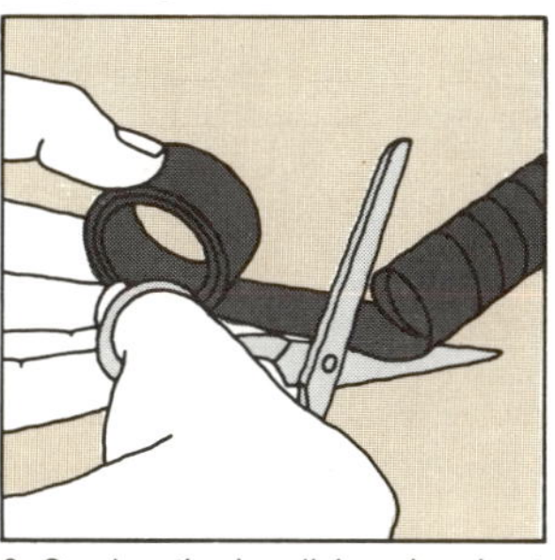

6 Overlap the handlebars by about $\frac{1}{4}$ in. (6 mm). Cut off neatly and tuck the surplus tape inside the tubing

Grips

Fitting new grips

Most handlebar grips are made from plastic or rubber. It is sometimes possible to slide the old grips off, but if they are firmly stuck to the handles they must be cut away. Use a knife to cut rubber grips, a small hacksaw to cut the harder plastic ones. Some plastic grips are in the form of a spiral: by twisting the grip one way, the spirals will open enabling it to be fitted easily. Rubber grips are stuck to the handles.

Materials: new handlebar grips; rubber solution.
Tools: junior hacksaw or a sharp knife; emery cloth.

1 Use a hacksaw to cut off plastic handlebar grips, taking care not to scratch the chrome

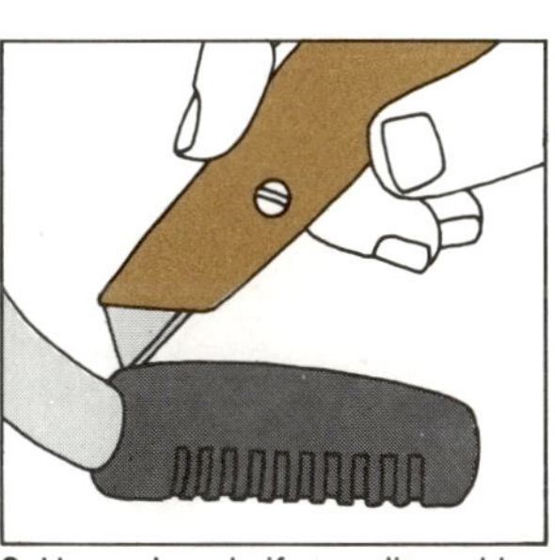

2 Use a sharp knife to split a rubber grip down the middle; then peel it back off the handlebar

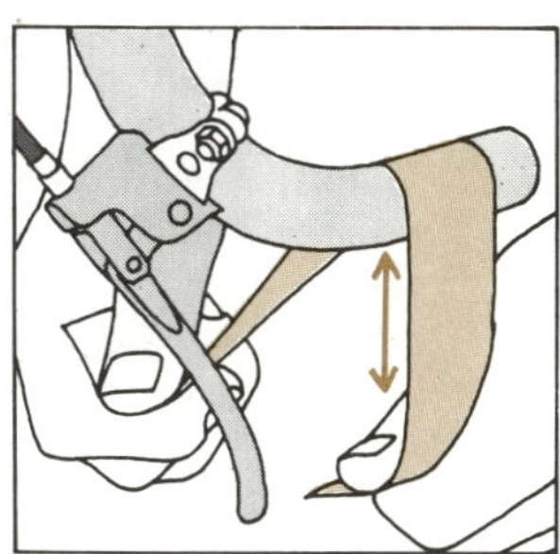

3 Clean old adhesive off the bars with emery cloth to just less than the length of the new grip

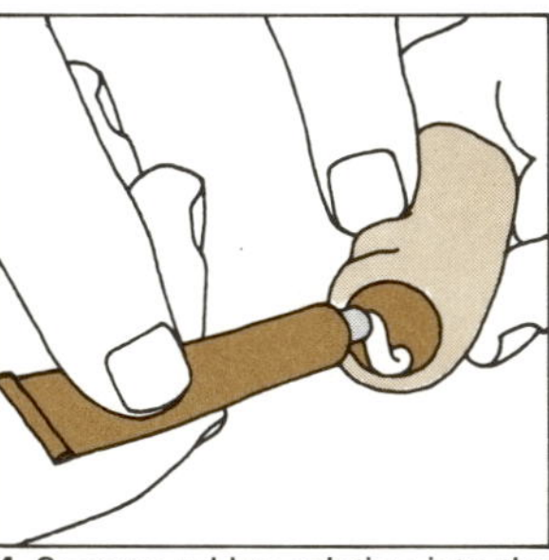

4 Squeeze rubber solution into the end of the grip. This helps it to slide on easily and holds it firm

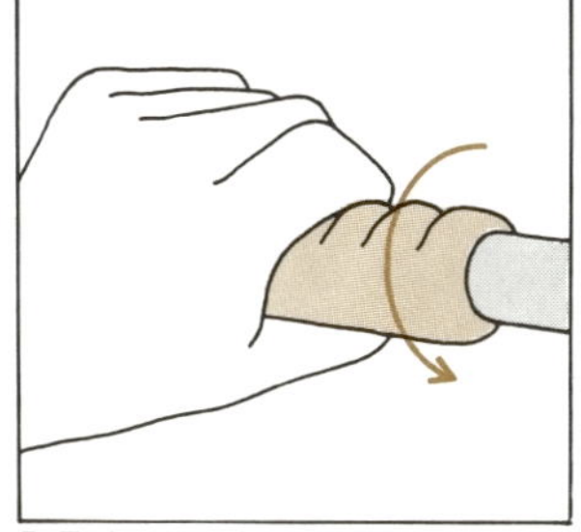

5 Twist the grip on to the bar, finishing with the finger grooves under the bar. Wipe off surplus solution

Checking and replacing bearings

If the handlebars turn with a harsh or clicking sound, the fork bearings need replacing.

The assembly below has bearing cups as an integral part of the cup housing fitted to the forks frame tube; another kind has separate cups sitting freely in the frame-tube housing.

Materials: ball bearings and bearing cups; grease.
Tools: spanner for handlebar centre bolt; thin-nosed pliers; spanner for locking-ring; hammer; long steel punch for bearing-cup removal; length of steel tube to fit over forks column; small steel punch; hide or plastic mallet.

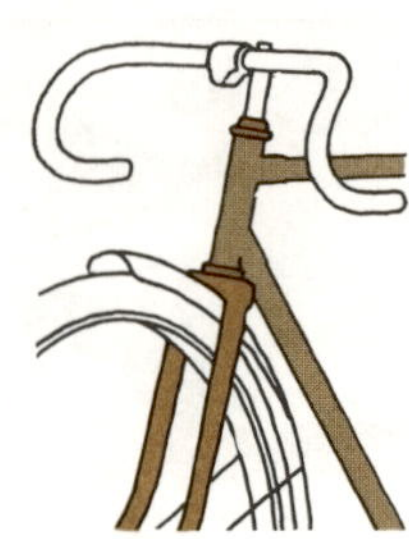

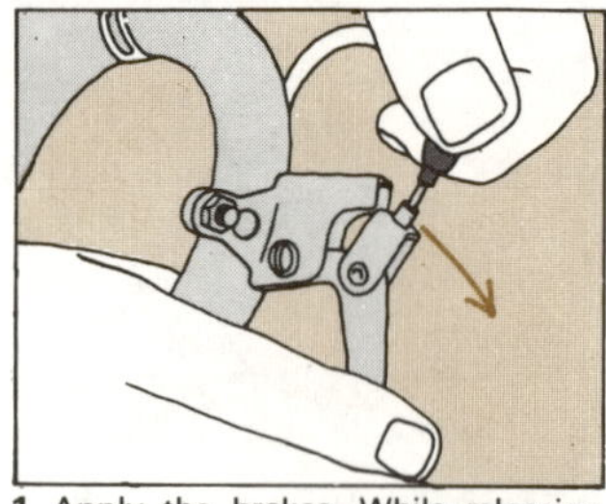

1 Apply the brakes. While releasing the lever, free the outer cable by withdrawing it from its stop in the head of the brake handle

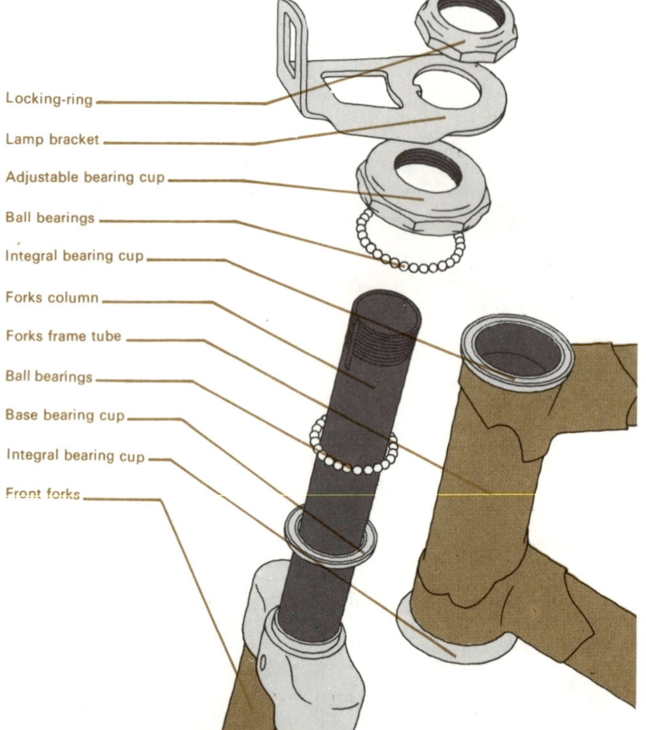

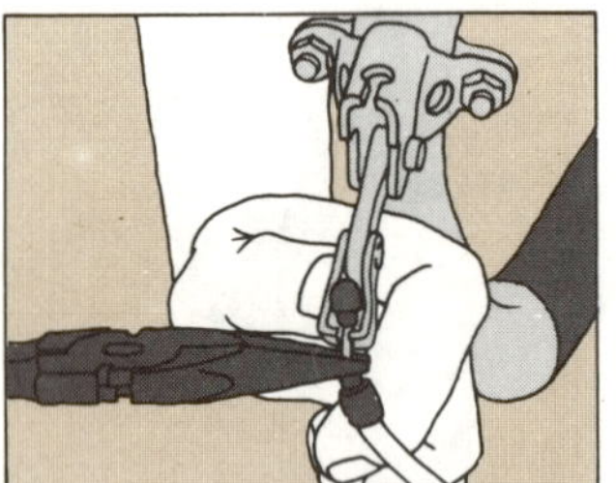

2 Pull back the outer cable to unhook the inner-cable nipple. With rod brakes, slacken the clevis adjusters and withdraw the rods

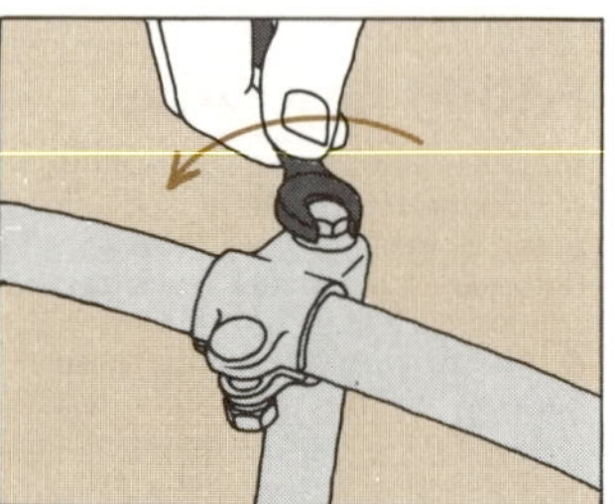

3 Undo the bolt in the centre of the handlebar stem anti-clockwise until it stands $\frac{1}{4}$ in. (6 mm), but no further, above the handlebars

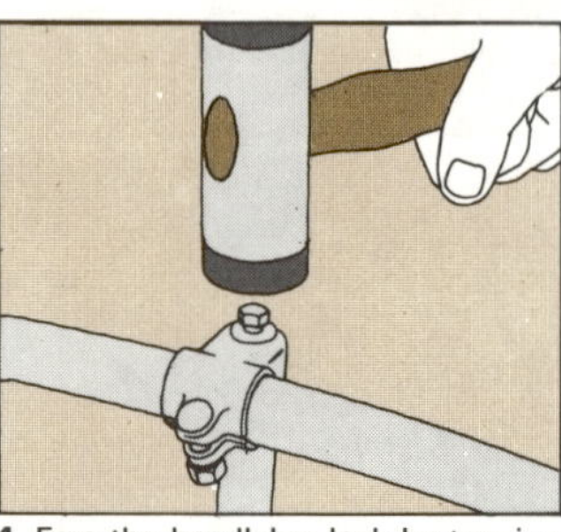

4 Free the handlebar lock by tapping down the centre bolt with a plastic mallet until it is flush with the top of the stem of the handlebars

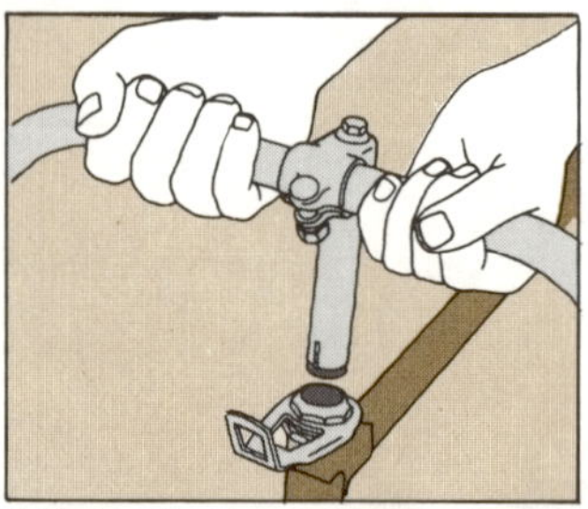

5 Twist the handlebars backwards and forwards, lifting them at the same time, until they are removed from the forks column

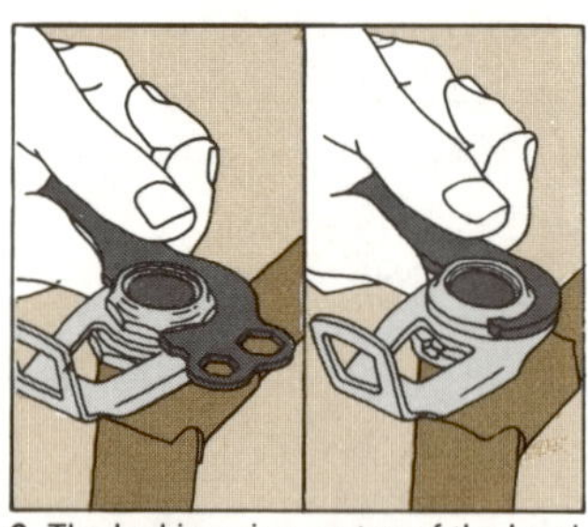

6 The locking-ring on top of the head bearing, which is either a hexagonal nut or a slotted C nut, can now be unscrewed with a suitable spanner

7 Remove the locking-ring, and the cycle-lamp bracket if one is fitted, to gain access to the adjustable bearing cup at the top of the column

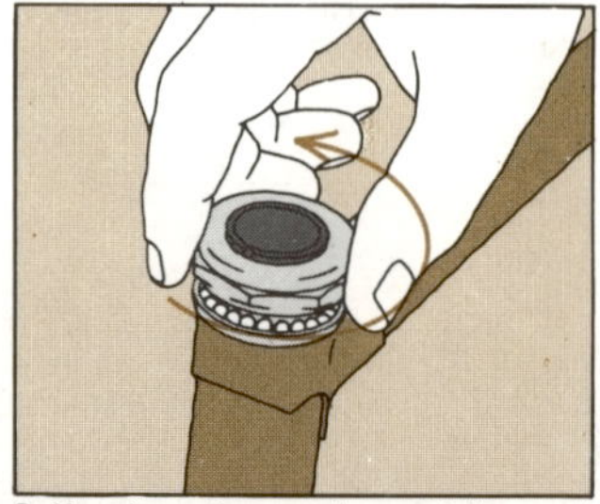

8 Keeping the cycle upright and steady, carefully unscrew the top adjustable bearing cup in an anti-clockwise direction

9 Take out the ball bearings from the integral cup and clean both cups. If the bearings show signs of wear buy new ones of the same size

Front forks

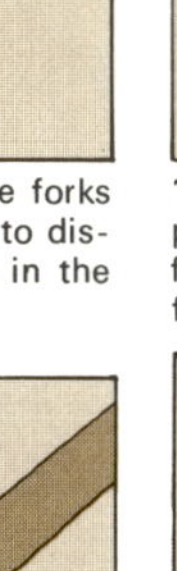

10 Lift the cycle frame off the forks tube. Take particular care not to disturb or lose the ball bearings in the lower race

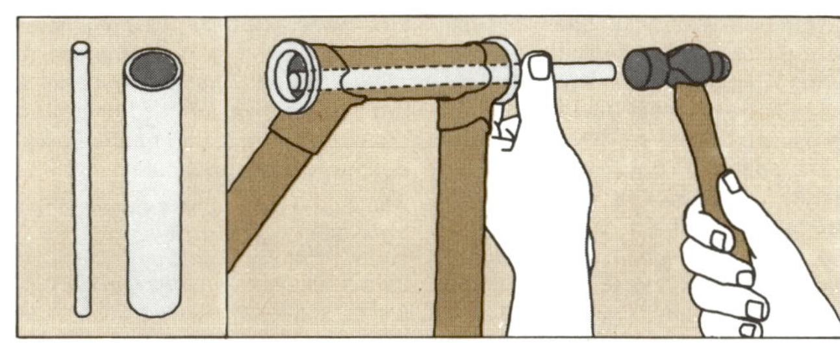

11 Two items are needed for removing and replacing bearing cups: a solid punch longer than the cycle-frame tube and a hollow tube, longer than the forks column, to fit over the column. Place the solid punch against the cup flange and hit with a hammer to expel either of the frame-fitted cups

12 Fit the new integral-type bearing cup into the cycle-frame tube. It must sit squarely to avoid causing damage to the frame

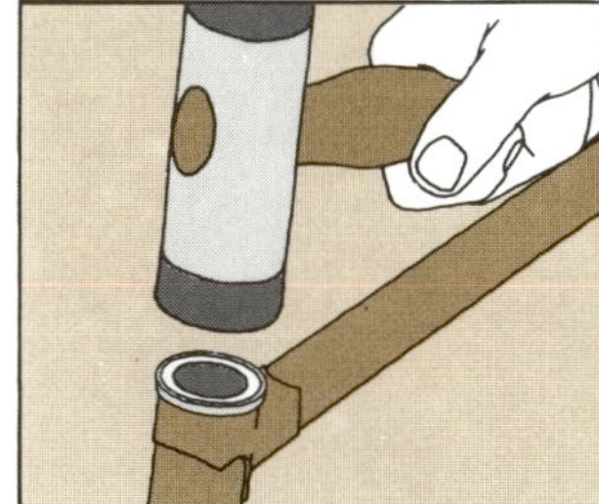

13 Use a hide or plastic mallet, or a hammer and hardwood block, to drive the bearing cup into the tube. Even seating is essential

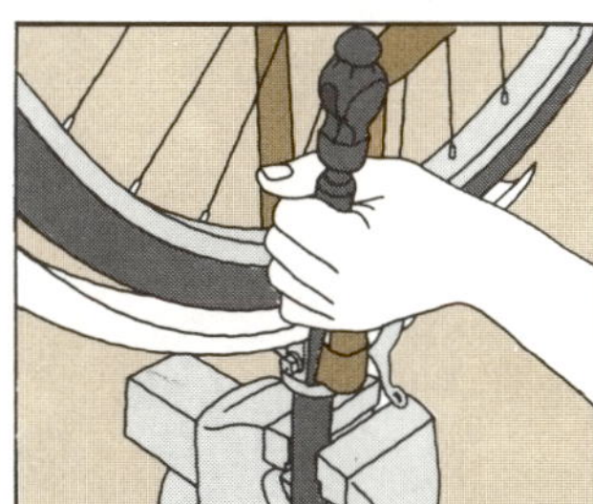

14 The bearing cup at the base of the front forks fits tightly over a shoulder on the column. Drive off the cup with a hammer and punch

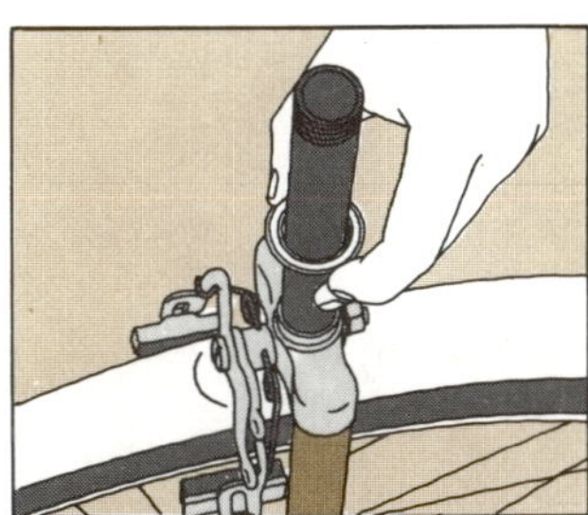

15 Clean the forks column, in particular the boss on which the bearing cup fits. Drop the new cup over the column and on to the boss

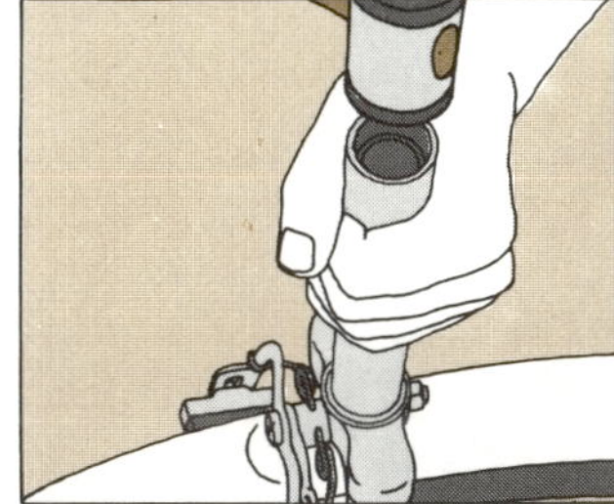

16 To fix the cup, slip the tubing, which should not be wide enough to slip into the bearing cup, over the column and tap with the mallet

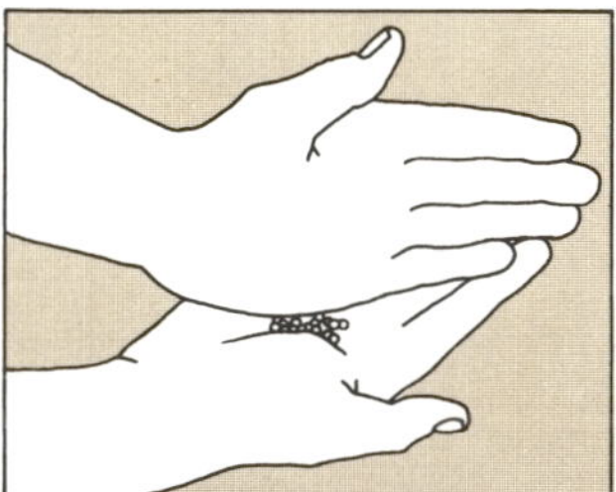

17 Wash the ball bearings from the lower race with those from the upper race in paraffin. Dry between the palms of the hands

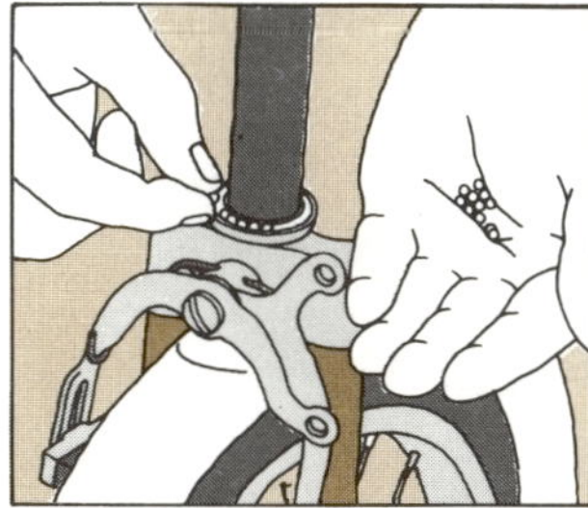

18 Grease the base bearing cup and replace the balls. If fitting new ones, check that they are correct in size and number

19 Grease the upper base bearing cup and lower the cycle frame over the forks column, taking care not to disturb the ball bearings

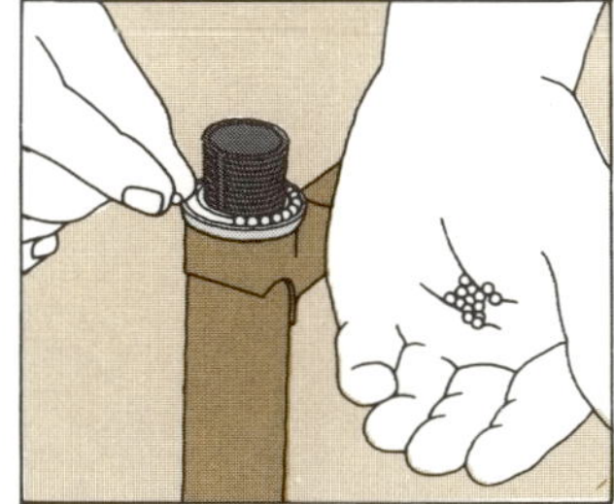

20 With the bearing cup on the upper fork greased, replace its ball bearings, again taking care to fit the right size and number of balls

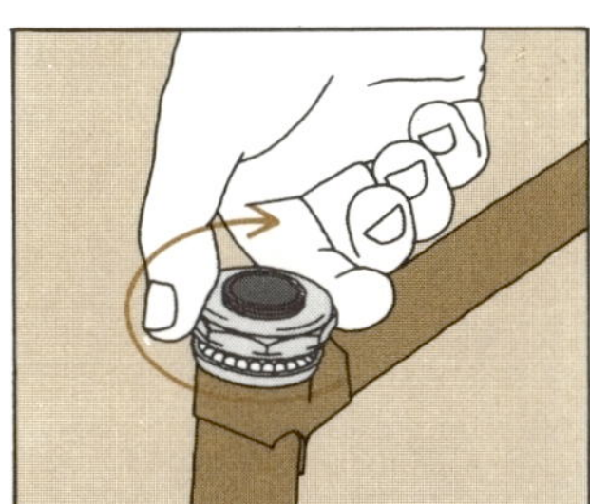

21 Screw the adjustable bearing cup on to the forks tube. Tighten until there is no more play and the fork bearings are moving freely

22 Replace the lamp bracket, with its tongue slotted in the column groove. Hold the adjustable cup firm and replace the locking-ring

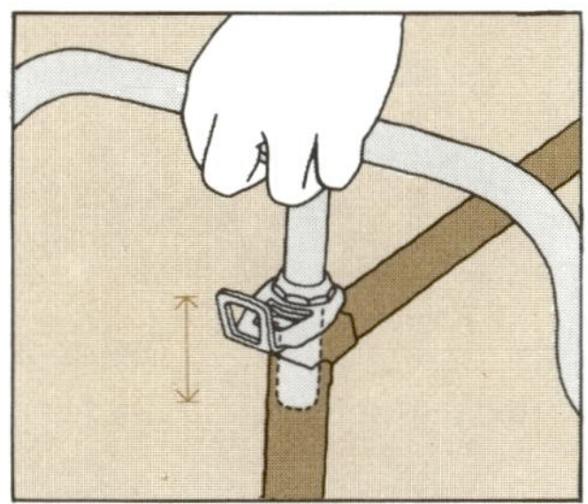

23 Replace the handlebars with at least $2\frac{1}{2}$ in. (65 mm) of their stem inside the forks column. Tighten the handlebar nut; replace the brakes

Checking and replacing bearings

A worn bottom-bracket bearing gives a rough or grating sensation when turned. Replace the balls as soon as this is noticed, otherwise the rest of the assembly may be damaged.

The bearing has two cups, a spindle with cones, a lock-ring and ball bearings. The fixed right-hand cup, behind the chain wheel crank, slackens in a clockwise direction: the other cup, which is adjustable and held by a lock-ring, is slackened anti-clockwise. The bearings are generally, but not always, $\frac{1}{4}$ in. (6 mm) in diameter. Bottom-bracket spindles are not standard in length, so take the old parts along for comparison when buying replacements.

Materials: a replacement spindle; left and right-hand cups; bearings; grease.
Tools: hammer; hardwood block; thin punch; spanner for cotter-pin nuts; hide mallet; C spanner for bearing lock-ring; cone or peg spanner.

1 Remove the chain by freeing its connecting link. Undo the nuts of the two crank cotter pins and remove the nuts and their washers

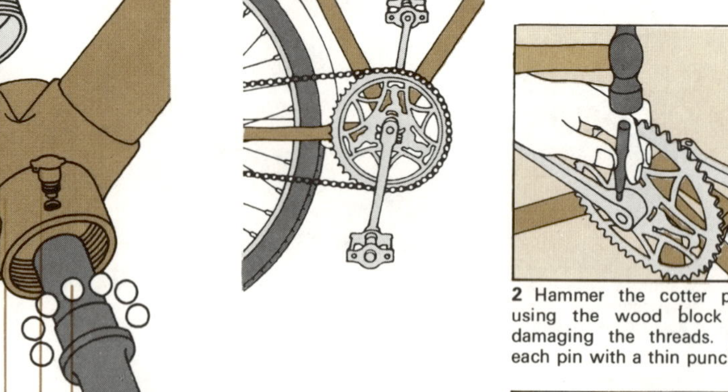

2 Hammer the cotter pins flush, using the wood block to avoid damaging the threads. Drive out each pin with a thin punch

3 Take off the crank wheel. If it is tight, hold the other crank lever and twist the wheel off the bottom-bracket spindle

4 If the left-hand crank lever is tight, tap it off with a soft-headed hammer or mallet, striking the lever close to its centre boss

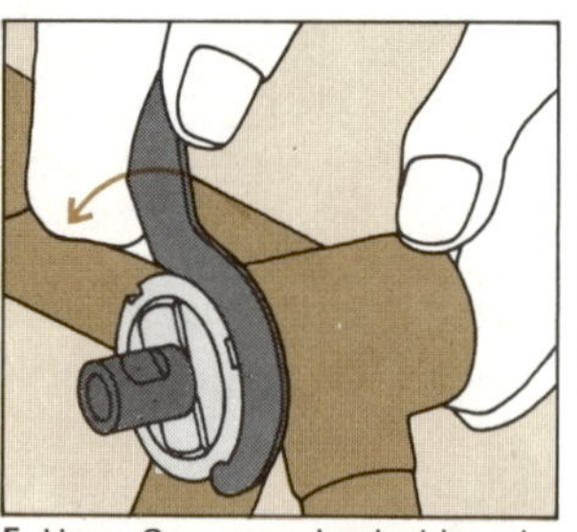

5 Use a C spanner, hooked into the notches of the lock-ring, to undo the ring. This unscrews in an anti-clockwise direction

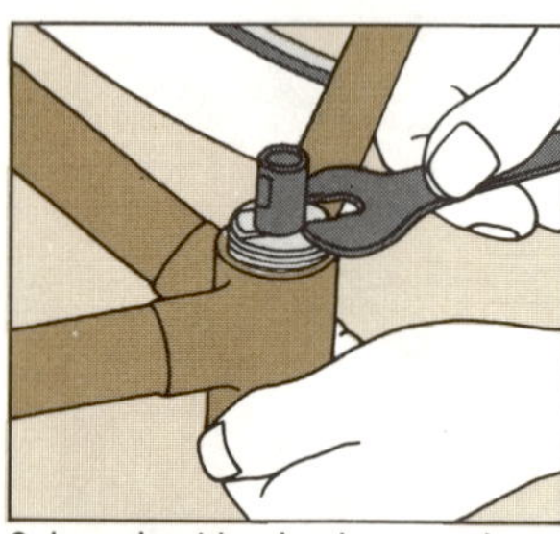

6 Lay the bicycle down and unscrew the adjustable cup. Hold the spindle against the cup as the cup is being removed

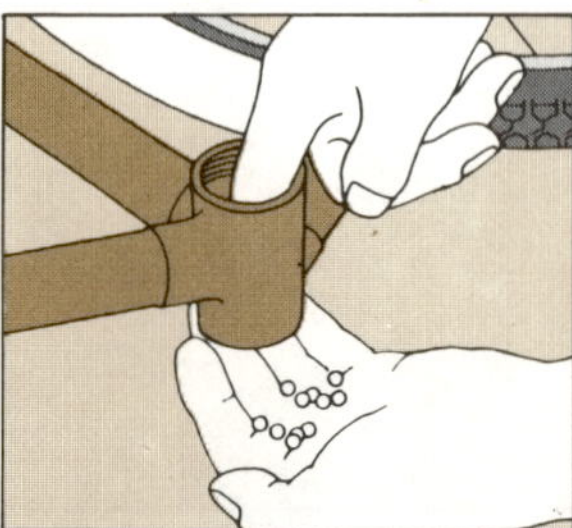

7 Draw out the spindle and cup, using one hand to catch the ball bearings. If any balls are stuck inside the hub, poke them free

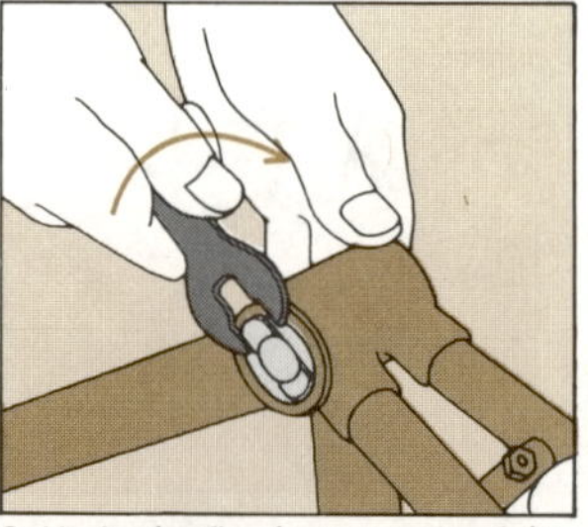

8 Undo the fixed cup on the right-hand side of the bracket in a clockwise direction. Remove the lubrication nipple if one is fitted

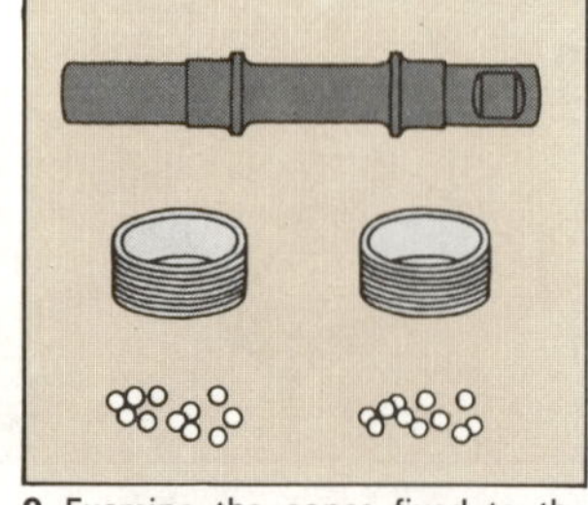

9 Examine the cones fixed to the spindle, the two cups and the ball bearings. Renew any parts that show signs of wear

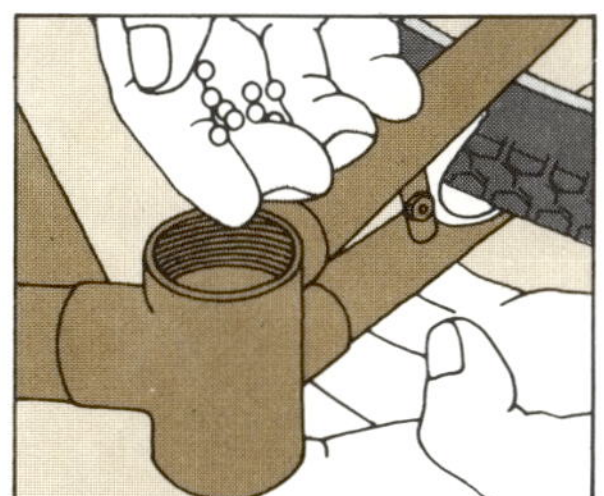

10 Refit the fixed cup and grease it. With a finger in the hole, replace the right number of bearings to sit evenly inside the cup

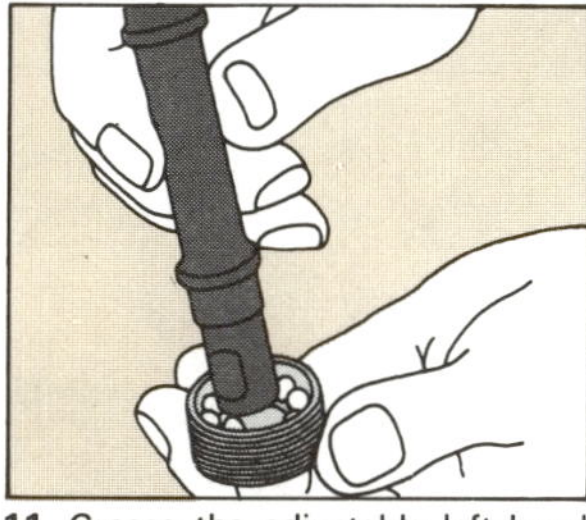

11 Grease the adjustable left-hand cup and replace the ball bearings. Place the shorter end of the spindle in position in the cup

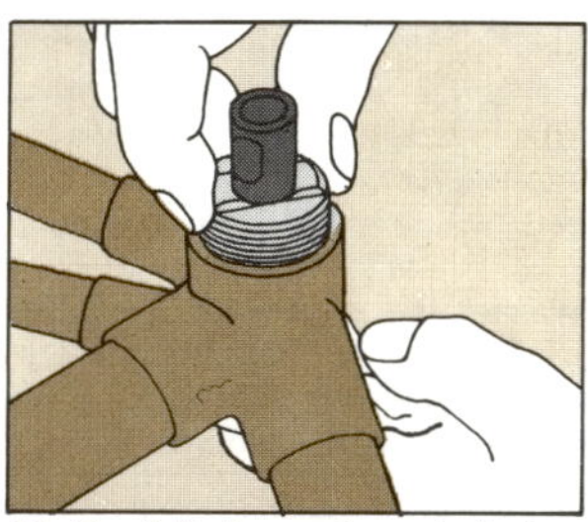

12 Carefully lower the spindle into the housing, making sure that the ball bearings at the other end are not disturbed. Screw the cup home

13 Tighten the cup clockwise to eliminate end play of the spindle, while still allowing it to revolve freely in the bearing

14 When the cup has been adjusted to its correct position, hold it with the spanner and tighten up the lock-ring to secure it

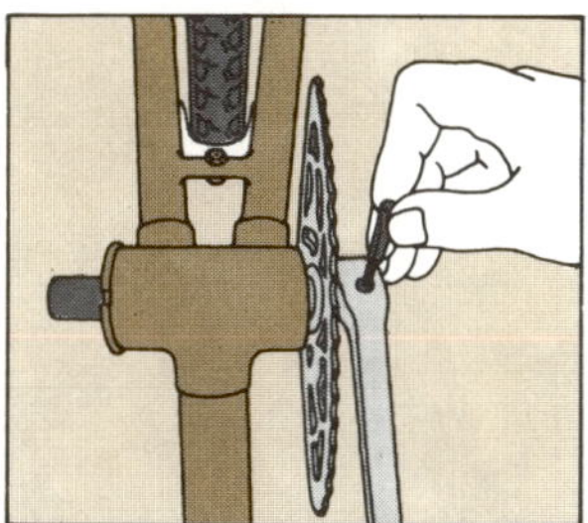

15 Refit the crank levers: the one with the chain wheel fits the longer right-hand side of the spindle. Replace the cotter pins

Adjusting and replacing cotter pins

A cotter pin needs adjusting or replacing if the crank lever is a loose fit on the spindle. This shows when riding if the lever drops forward slightly as it passes the upper vertical position.

Adjust by tapping the pin further in, filing it if necessary. If, after adjustment, the unthreaded end of the pin is about flush with the crank lever, so that at the other end the thread sticks out too far for the nut to be tightened, fit a new cotter pin.

Materials: new cotter pin (standard size), with washer and nut.
Tools: spanner to fit nut; file; hammer; hardwood block; vice.

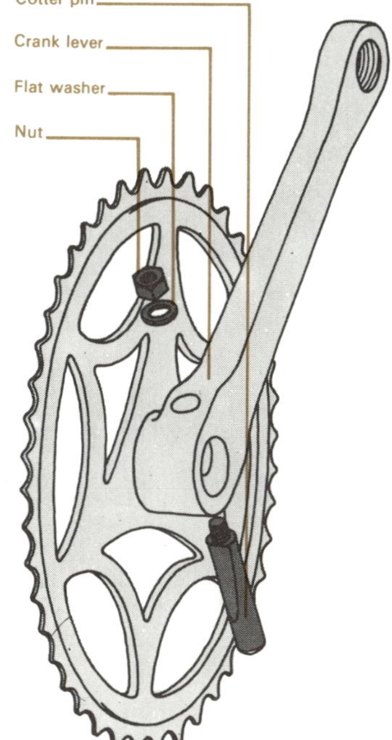

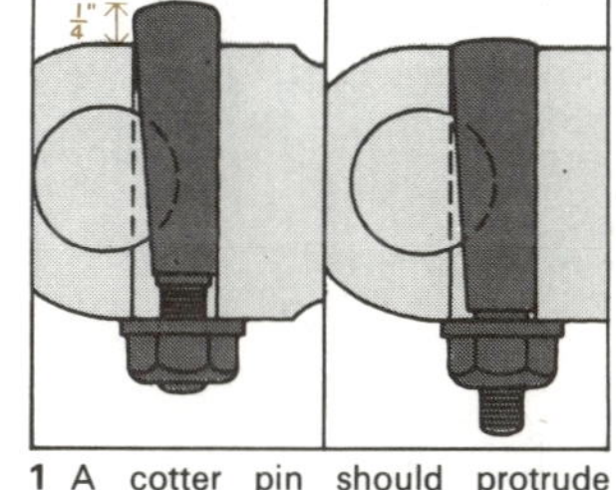

1 A cotter pin should protrude about $\frac{1}{4}$ in. (6 mm) from the crank (left). The pin on the right cannot be adjusted and must be replaced

2 Supporting the crank with a block, hit the new pin with a hammer. Enough thread must be exposed to take the washer and fit the nut

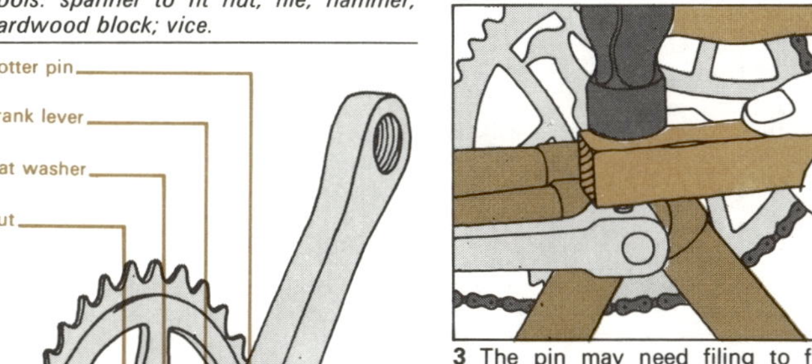

3 The pin may need filing to fit. When tapping it out, a hardwood block held between the pin and the hammer safeguards the thread

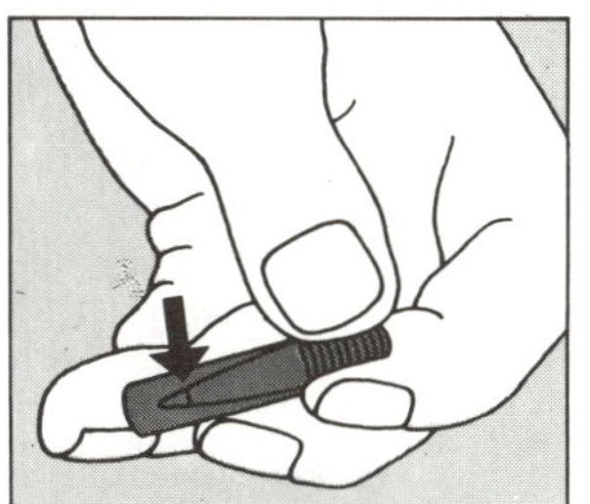

4 Score marks on the flat side of the cotter pin, caused by friction inside the crank when driving in the pin, will indicate where to file the pin

5 With the pin in a vice, flat face uppermost and just clear of the vice jaws, file evenly to remove the score marks. Refit the pin in the crank

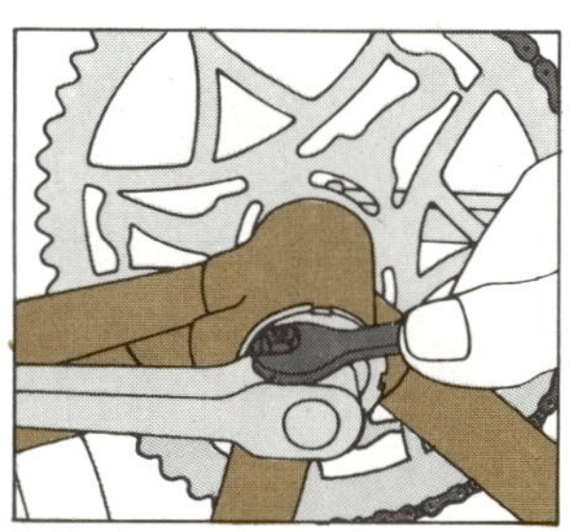

6 Fit the washer and nut on the replaced pin, tightening the nut clockwise. Make sure the thread of the pin fits the nut

Pedals

Bearings

Renewing the bearings

Pedal bearings wear in time if not oiled regularly. In use, their action begins to feel rough to the feet.

A pedal has a spindle with a fixed cone at the inner end, an adjustable cone, a lock-washer and a lock-nut. Because the ball bearings sit in cups which are an integral part of the pedal, new pedals must be fitted if the cups become worn.

Materials: medium-grade grease; new components as necessary.
Tools: pedal spanner; spanner for the lock-nut; screwdriver; vice.

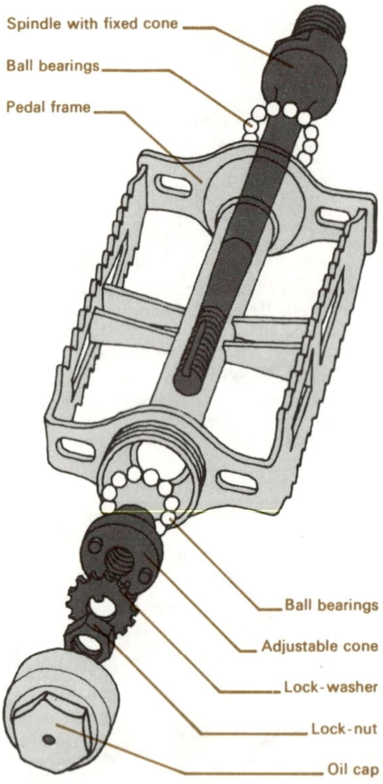

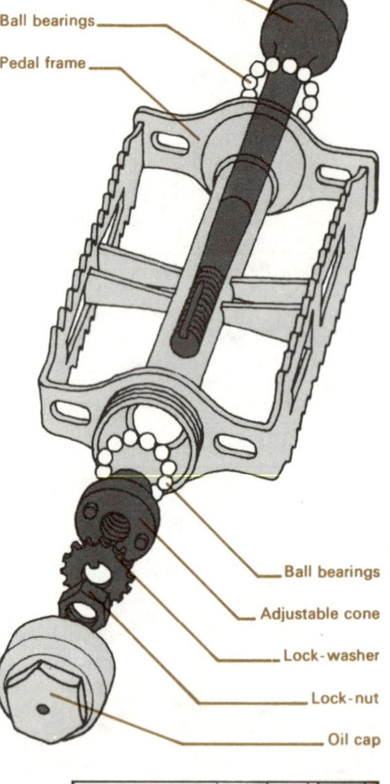

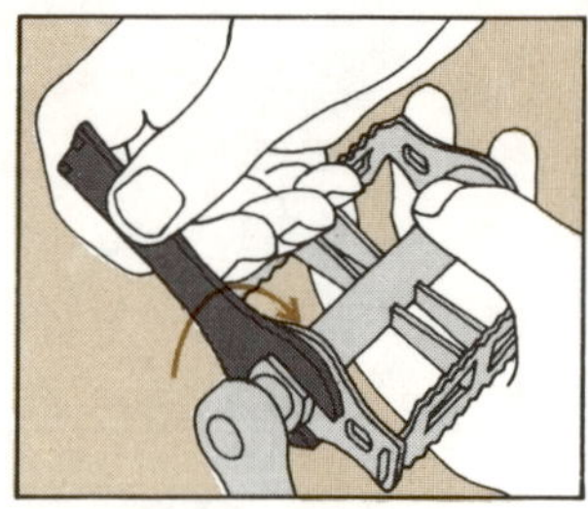

1 Remove the pedals from the crank levers. The right-hand pedal is undone as shown; turn the other pedal spindle the opposite way

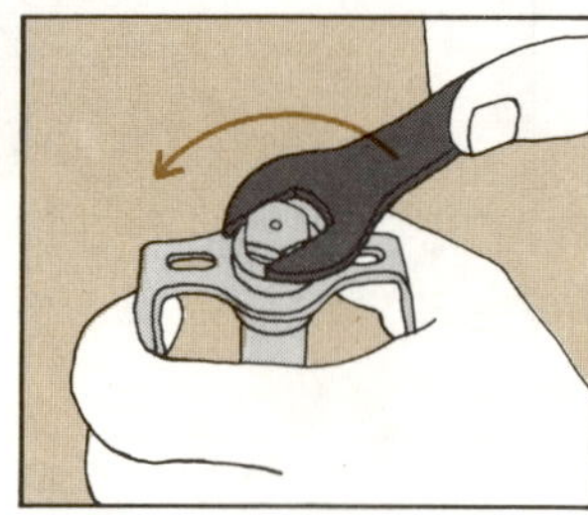

2 With the pedal spindle held in a vice above the threaded end, remove the oil cap from the outside plate with a spanner

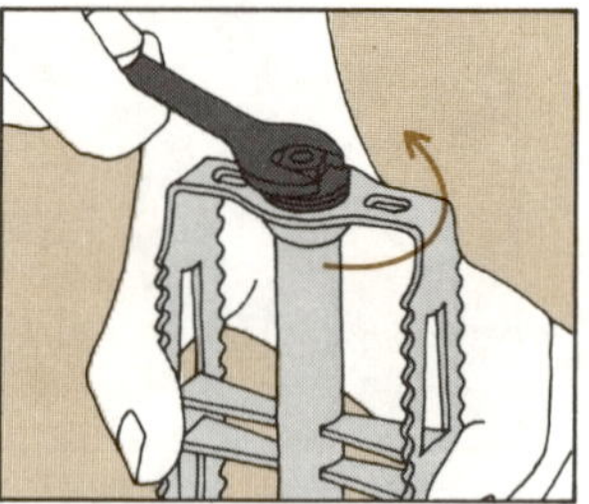

3 Immediately below the oil cap is the outer bearing lock-nut. Remove this nut and the lock-washer beneath the lock-nut

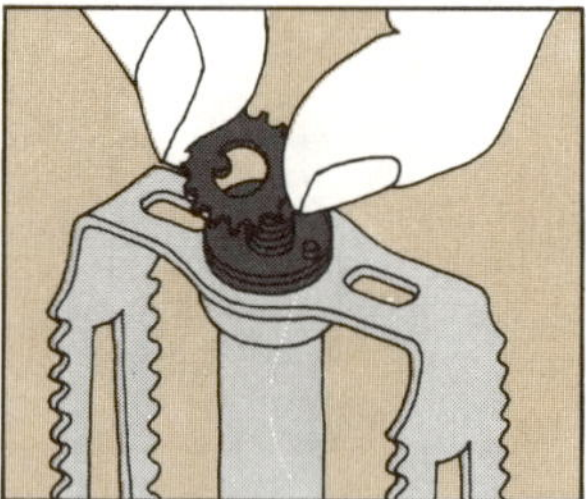

4 The washer has a peg fitting a groove in the spindle and serrations that lock over two pegs on the face of the adjustable cone

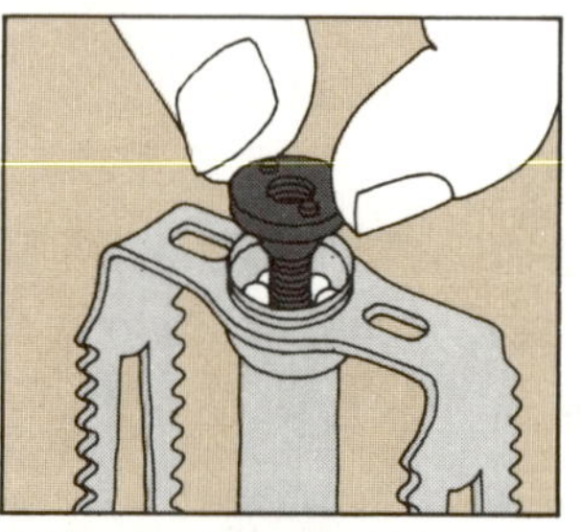

5 Unscrew the adjustable cone, using its two pegs as lever points for a rigid edge if the cone has been secured more than finger-tight

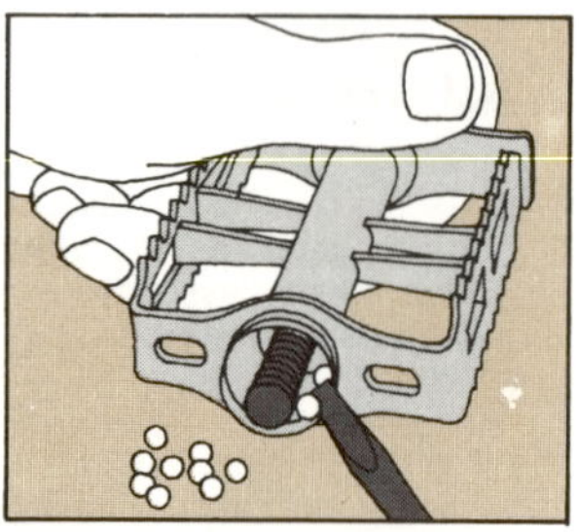

6 Remove the ball bearings from the outer cup, holding the spindle in place to secure the rest of the ball bearings at the other end

7 Withdraw the spindle and take the ball bearings from the inner cup. Count the balls from both cups as a guide to replacement

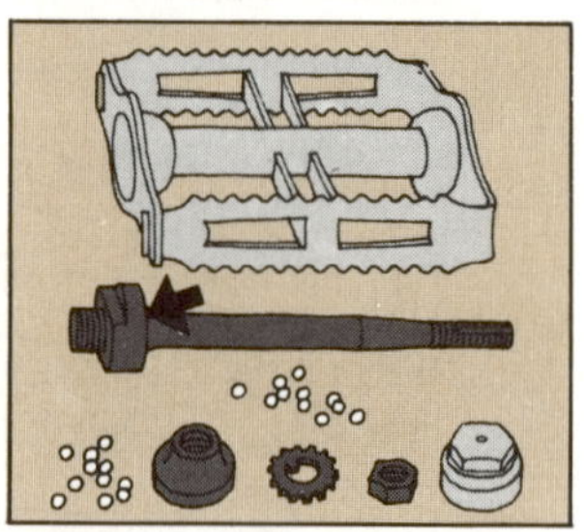

8 Clean and check the parts. If the fixed cone is worn, replace the spindle. Renew the balls if they are pitted or rusted

9 Grease the inner cup, partly insert the spindle, and replace the balls. Push the spindle home and invert the pedal

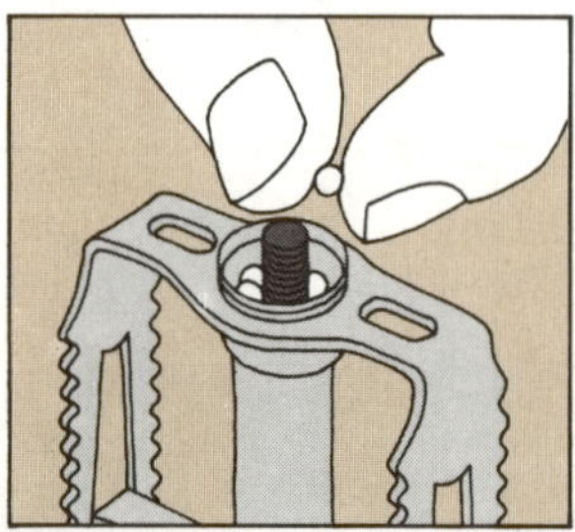

10 Grease the outer cup and refit the other ball bearings in the cup, making sure that they fit snugly and evenly round the spindle

11 Screw on the adjustable cone, tightening until the pedal is stiff. Then ease it off slightly until the pedal turns freely

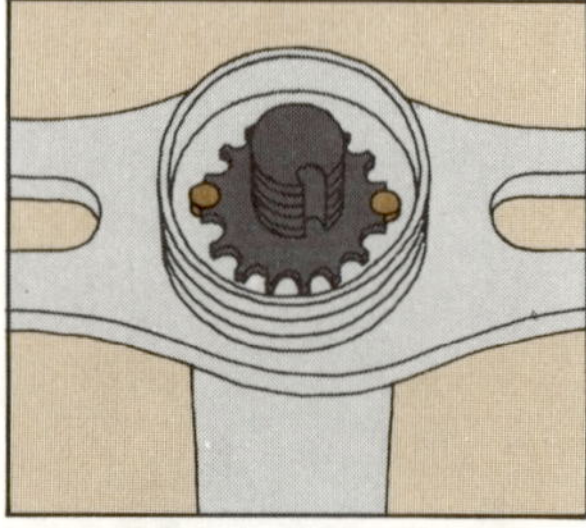

12 Refit the lock-washer, with its serrations locked against the pegs of the adjustable cone. Replace the lock-nut and oil cap

Fitting new mudguards

Mudguards on sports cycles are generally made of plastic; those on roadsters are usually steel. The method of fitting is basically the same; but whereas the stays on a plastic mudguard (shown in the picture sequence) fit lugs on the sides of the cycle frame, those on a steel mudguard (below) are usually secured on the wheel spindles inside the washers of the wheel nuts.

Materials: pair of mudguards to suit the wheel diameter.
Tools: spanners to fit mudguard nuts; small hacksaw; pliers; screwdriver.

STEEL MUDGUARDS

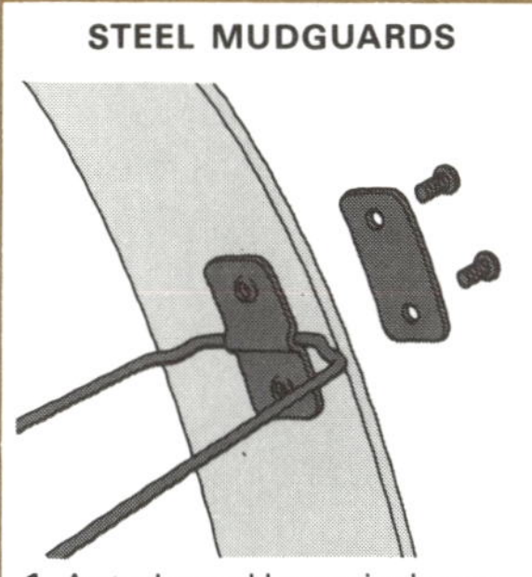

1 A steel guard has a single one-piece stay held on the inside by a plate and bolts

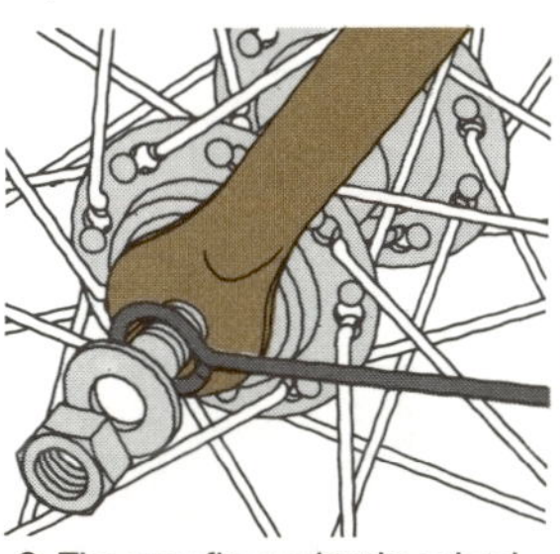

2 The stay fits under the wheel-hub nuts, with a washer between the nut and stay

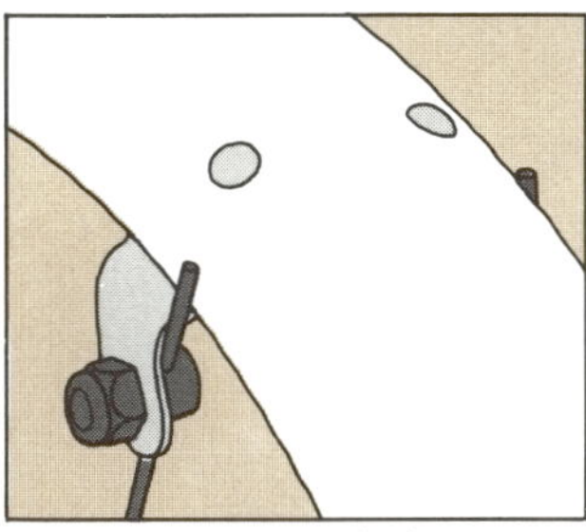

1 On plastic mudguards the stays are fixed to the guard brackets by small clevis pins and nuts

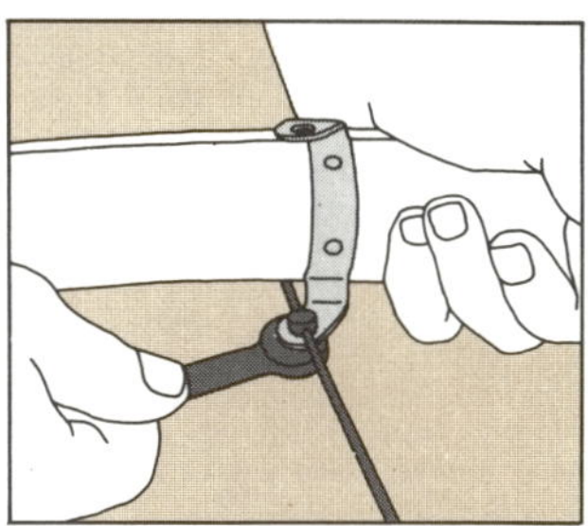

2 Fit the pins to the brackets, with the nuts on the outside and the stay holes on the inside

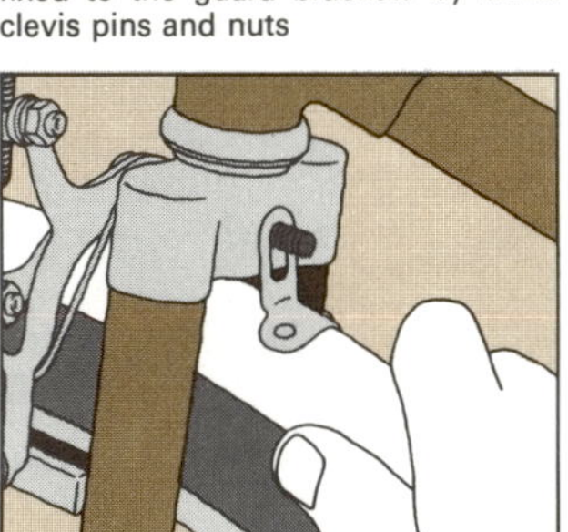

3 Slide the front guard through the forks until the clip fits on the bolt at the rear of the forks

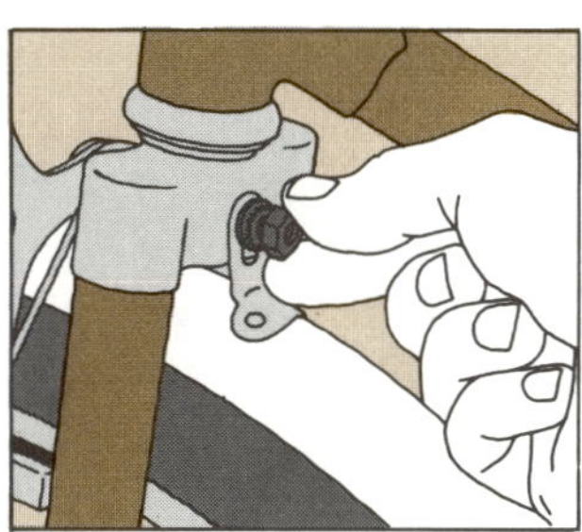

4 Fit a flat washer and a star lock-washer to the bolt. Screw on the nut but do not tighten yet

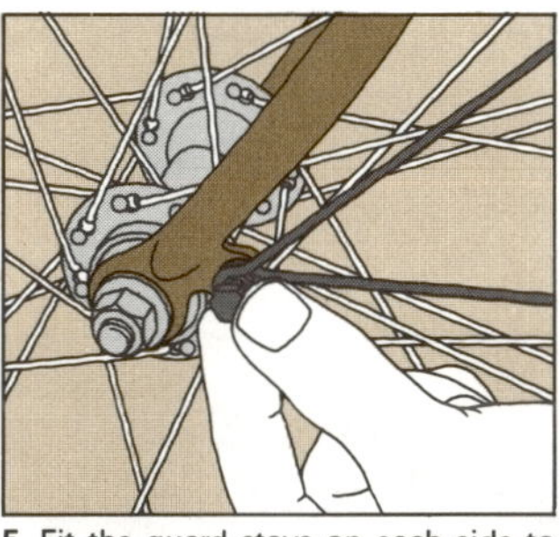

5 Fit the guard stays on each side to the fork bolt and screw the bolt finger-tight into its lug

6 With the clevis nuts loosened, adjust the mudguard to get it parallel with the tyre. Tighten all nuts

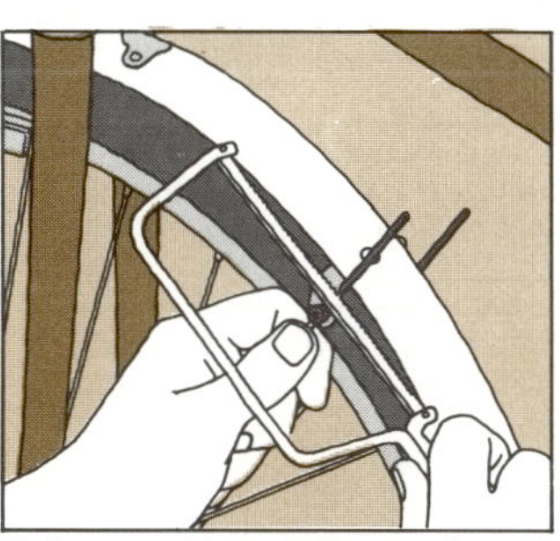

7 Cut two-thirds of the way through the protruding stays about 1 in. (25 mm) above each clevis pin

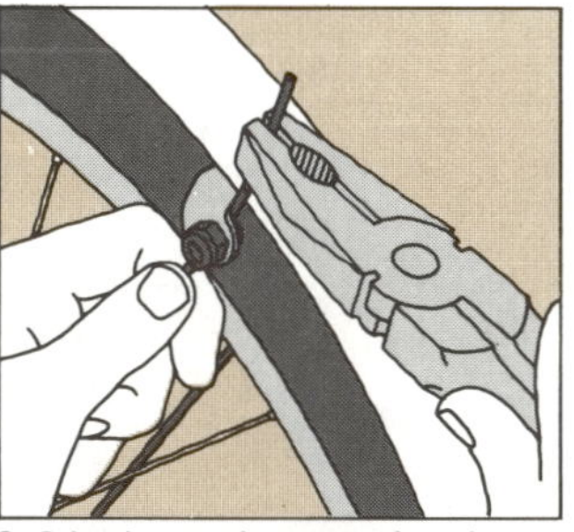

8 Grip the surplus part of each stay with a pair of pliers and bend at the cut to make a clean break

9 Now slide the rear mudguard through the forks. Take off the brake caliper if more room is needed

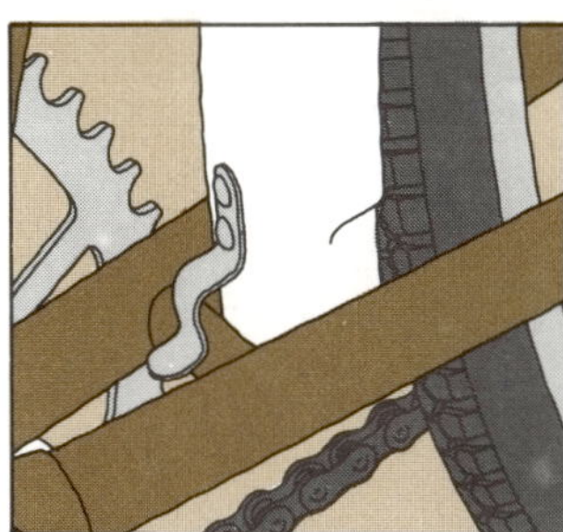

10 Press the fixed clip on the bottom of the guard over the tube between the horizontal forks

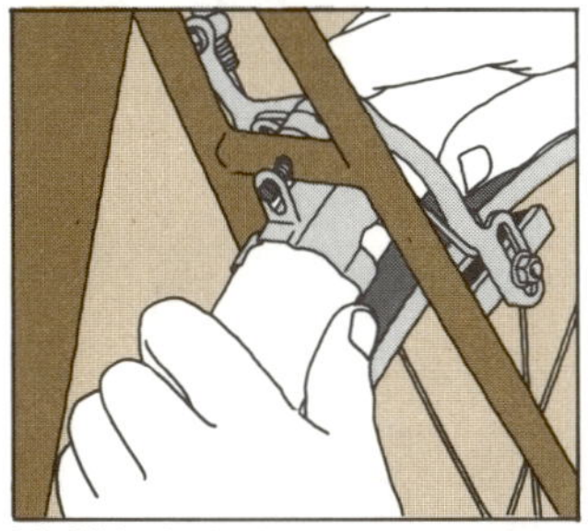

11 Slide the bridge between the vertical frame tubes. The bridge eye fits the brake-caliper centre bolt

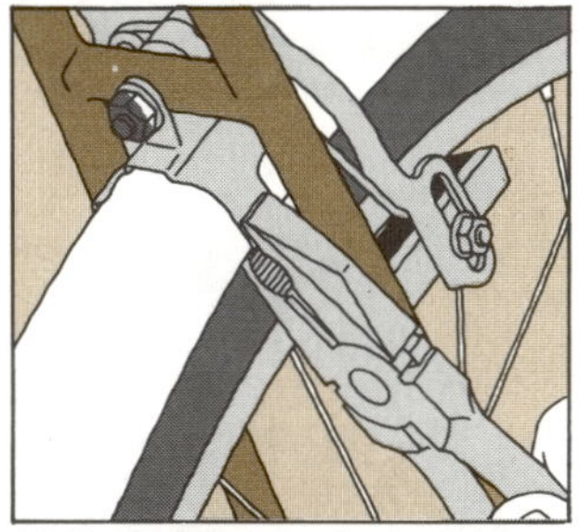

12 Tighten the nut, adjust and tighten the stays, then bend the bridge around the mudguard edges

Crankset

Removing and greasing

Removing and greasing a one-piece crankset

One-piece cranksets—which are fixed to the wheel—are found on Continental folding cycles and small-wheel cycles. The cranksets are not made of case-hardened metal, as are those on British cycles, and so they need to be kept in extra good order. Neglect will cause them to wear quickly and develop faults—when they must be replaced. This is a costly job and spare parts may be difficult to obtain. It is therefore advisable to check the crankset once every two weeks when the cycle is in regular use.

Materials: one-piece crankset.
Tools: spanner; grease; rag.

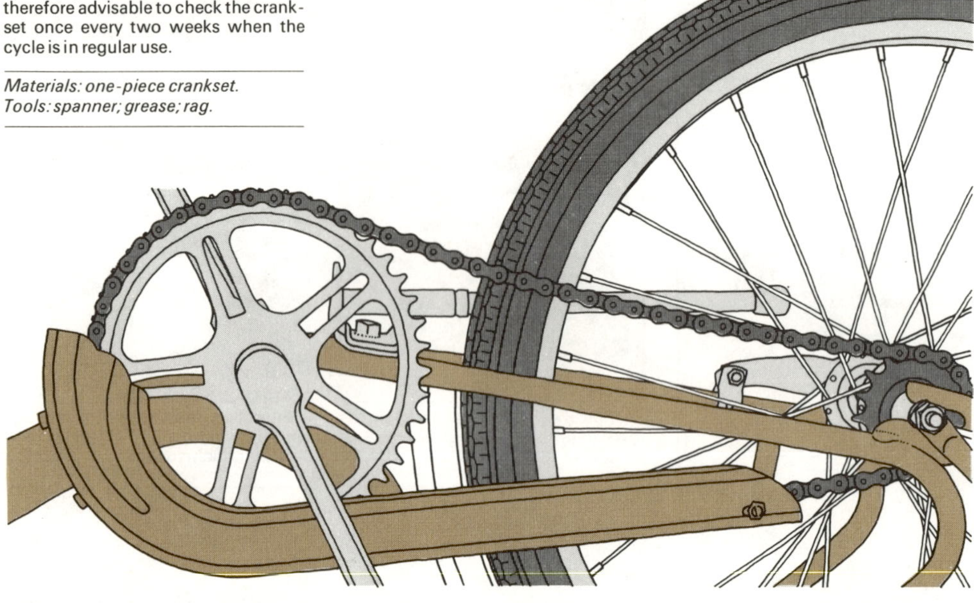

1 When chain guard is removed, turn the cycle upside-down and remove the cotter pin from the left-hand side.

2 Undo the lock-nut – turning to the left – and remove the washer and dustcap

3 Remove cone by hand. If necessary, use a spanner to remove the ring, and then take out the bearings

4 Remove the crankset, axle and right-hand bearing race. Clean the cones and bearing cup with a rag

5 Put grease on your forefinger and grease the bearing surfaces, cones and bearing races

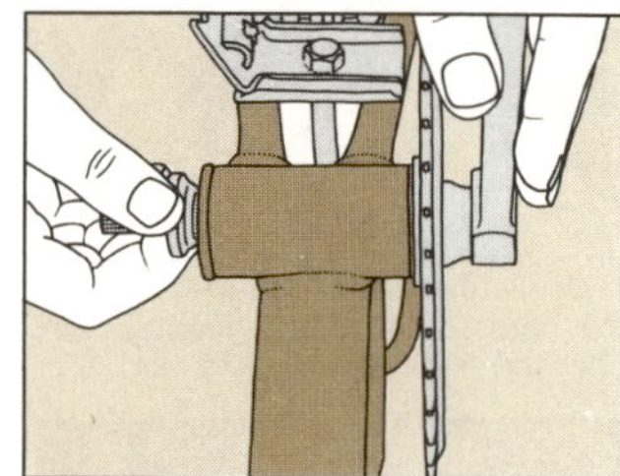

6 Replace the bearings and slide the axle and crankset in place from the right-hand side

7 Screw down cone by hand until tightly fixed. Replace washer and dustcap and then the lock-nut

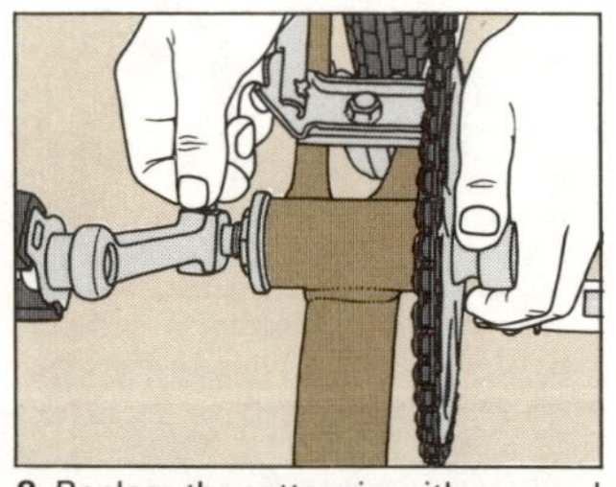

8 Replace the cotter pin with care and then make sure that the entire unit is securely in place

Removing a cotterless crankset

Cotterless cranksets, which are in regular use on sports cycles, should be cleaned once a year. To remove a cotterless crankset, first turn the cycle upside-down and then place a rag under the saddle.

Work on the right-hand side of the cycle and then on the left. The crankset is removed by a cotterless crank remover and is replaced by hand. The crankset is cleaned with paraffin or a commercial cleaning fluid.

Cycles with alloy cranks should have the lock-nut checked and tightened every 50 miles.

Materials: cotterless crankset.
Tools: cotterless crank extractor; spanner; screwdriver; cleaning fluid.

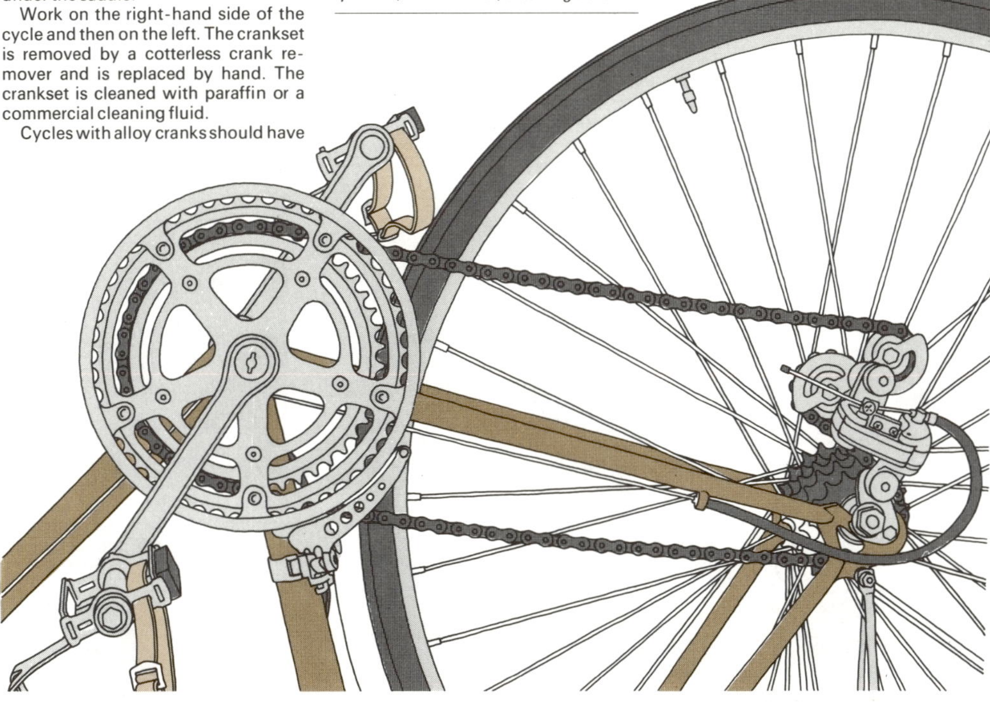

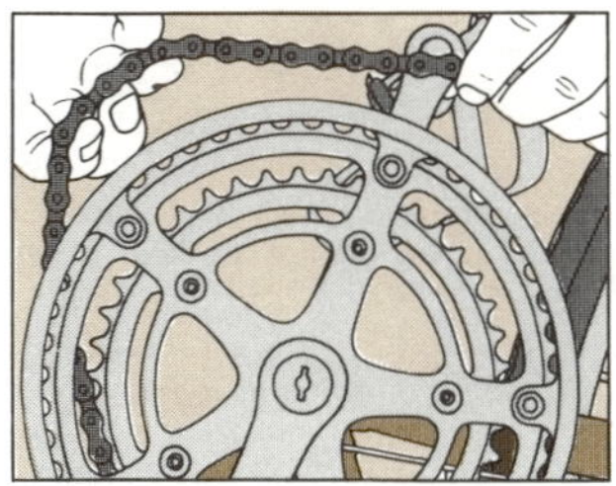

1 Turn the cycle upside-down and remove the chain from the chain wheel by hand

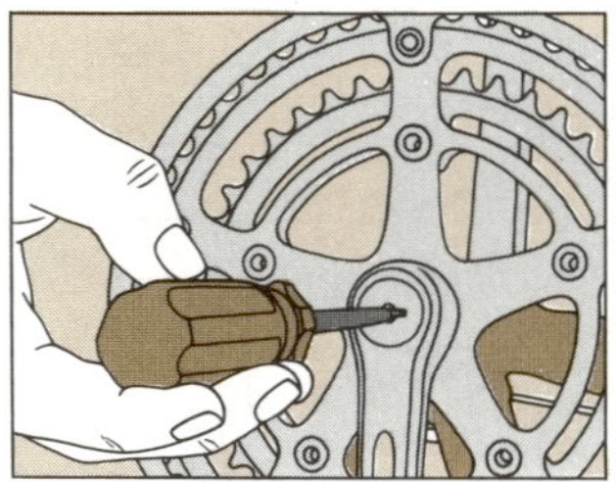

2 Remove the dustcaps on either side of the cranks, by the bottom bracket axle, exposing both nuts

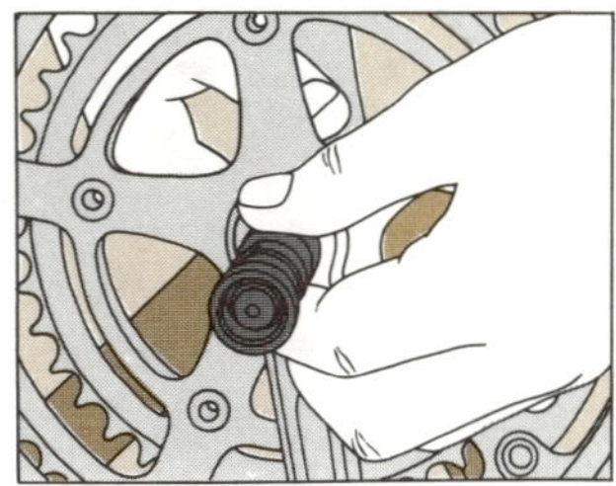

3 Use the cotterless crank extractor to loosen both the nuts. Then remove them from the axle

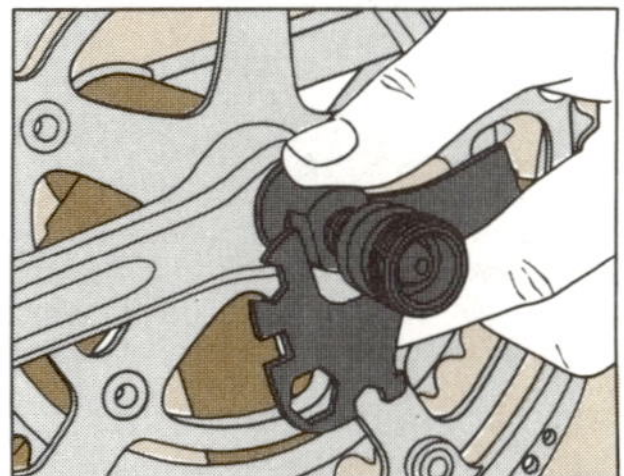

4 Carefully insert the threaded end of the crank extractor into the crank arm and screw it fully in

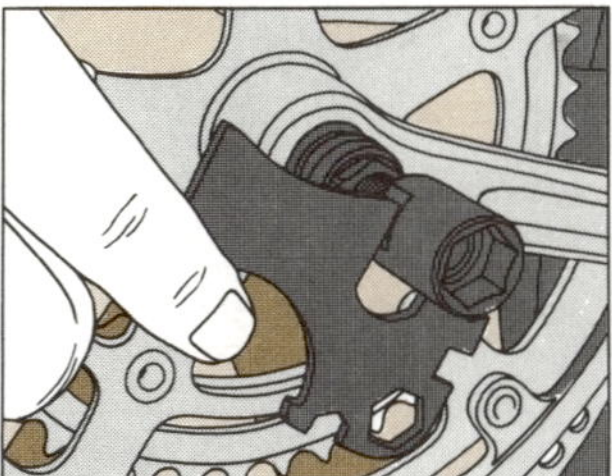

5 Tighten the other end of the crank extractor with the spanner. This releases the crank

6 Remove the crank and repeat the process on the other side of the cotterless crankset

7 Replace the cranks on either side of the axle by pushing them on by hand. Replace and tighten the nuts

Dynamos

Checking a tyre-driven unit

A conventional tyre-driven dynamo must be correctly positioned if it is to work well without wearing the tyre unduly. If, after adjustment, it fails to work, test both bulbs with a battery and test-leads. If these are sound, test the dynamo and cycle wiring and clean the bulb contacts.

Materials: bulbs and wire, as necessary.
Tools: spanner for dynamo bracket bolts; small screwdriver; test lamp made up from 6v bulb, bulb holder, bell wire and crocodile clips; ruler; straight-edge; fine emery cloth; battery.

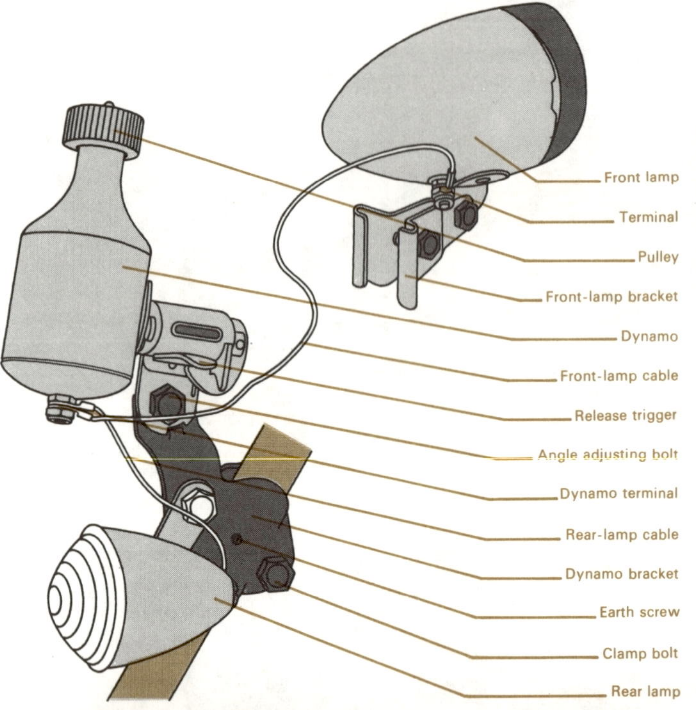

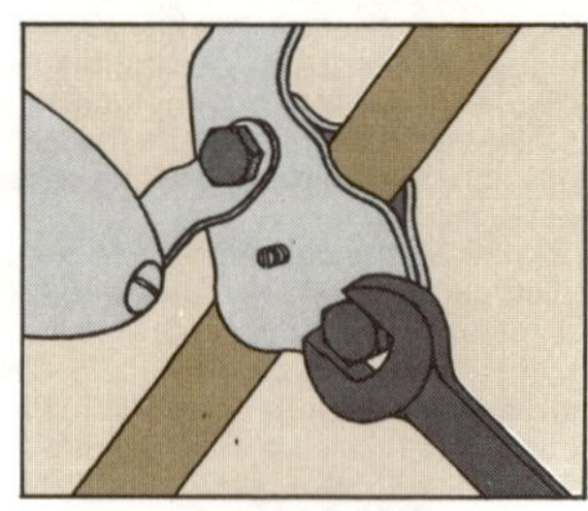

1 Loosen the two clamp bolts on the dynamo bracket, and the earth screw, just enough to allow the dynamo unit to be moved

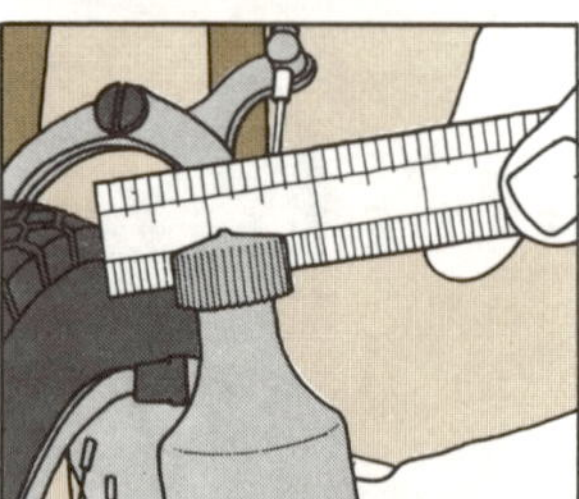

2 With the dynamo in the 'off' position, clearance between tyre and dynamo pulley should be $\frac{5}{8}$ in. (16 mm). Adjust if necessary

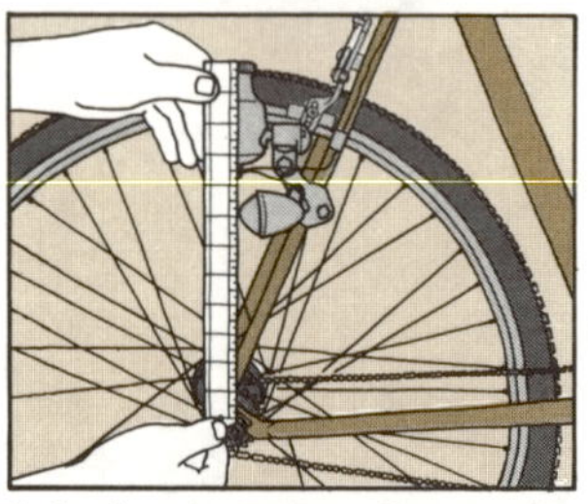

3 An imaginary centreline on the dynamo body should align with the hub centre. Adjust at the angle-adjusting bolt

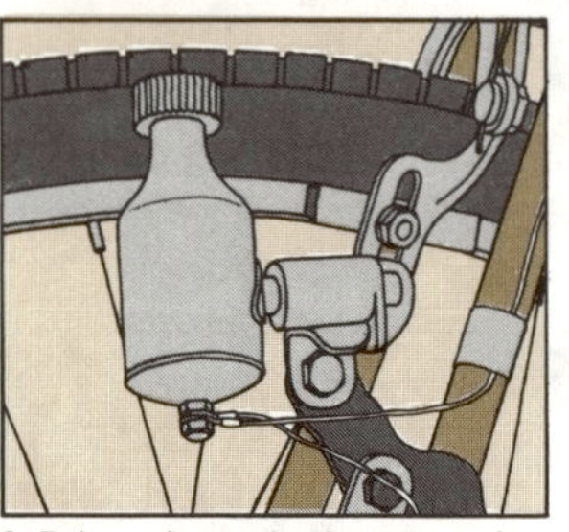

4 Raise or lower the dynamo so that the centre of the pulley contacts the tyre at a point slightly above the centre of the tyre wall

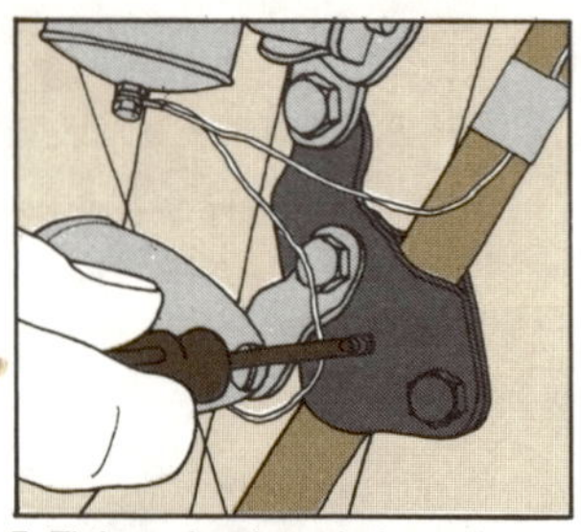

5 Tighten the clamp bolts and earth screw. If the unit still does not work, undo the leads on the two terminals at the base of the dynamo

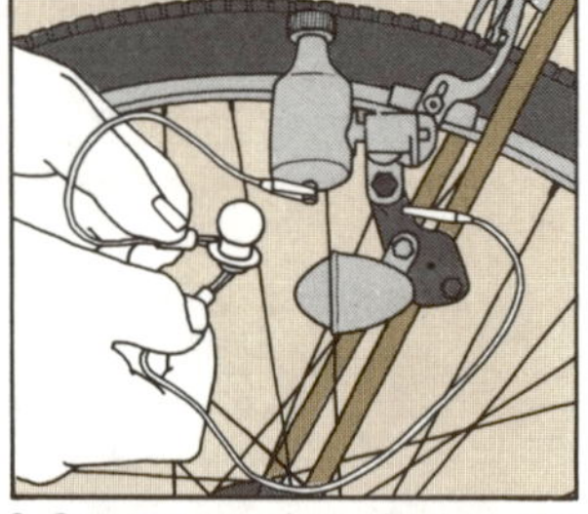

6 Connect one lamp lead to the bracket, the other to the dynamo terminal. The bulb should light when the wheel is spun with the dynamo on

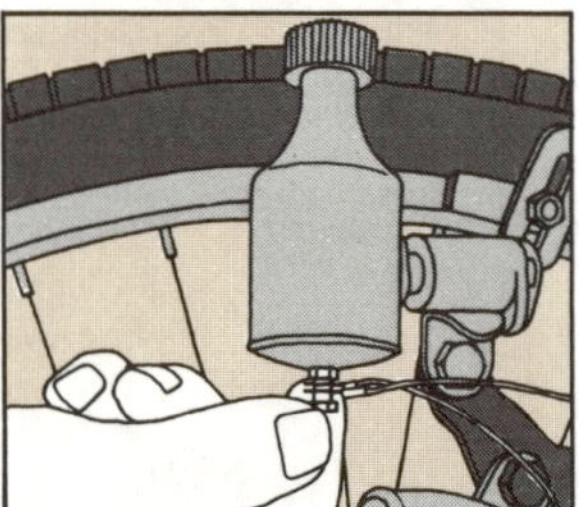

7 To test the cycle wiring, clean the terminals on the front and rear lamps. Refit the two leads to the terminal at the base of the dynamo

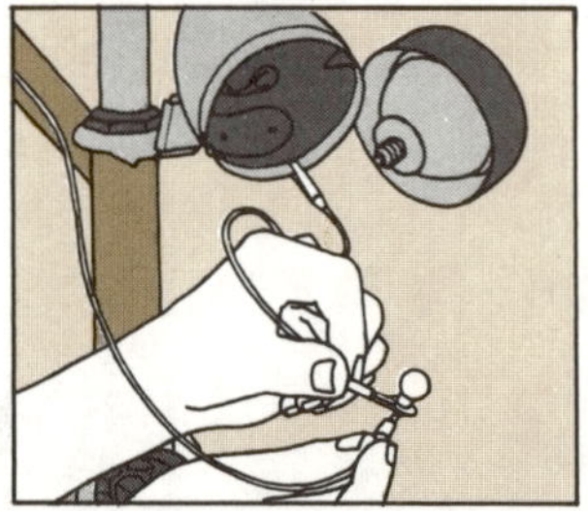

8 Test each cable in turn by connecting it to the test lamp and earthing the lamp's other wire. Test by spinning the wheel

9 Check the condition of the bulb contacts in both lamps. If they are dirty, rub the contact area with fine emery cloth

Testing and cleaning

A Dynohub generator is built into the front or rear-wheel hub. The unit should never be dismantled; this causes demagnetisation, even if the armature is removed for only a short period. If the unit includes batteries, remove them as soon as they are exhausted, otherwise they may cause corrosion.

When tracing a fault, check the bulbs first with a battery and test lamp. Check that all contacts are clean. If the unit still does not work, check the Dynohub, the switch contacts and the wiring. When testing the wiring, check that the switch is on.

Materials: bulbs, cables, batteries, as necessary. Tools: spanner for terminal nuts; test lamp made up of bulb, bulb holder, bell wire and crocodile clips; fine emery cloth.

SWITCH ASSEMBLY

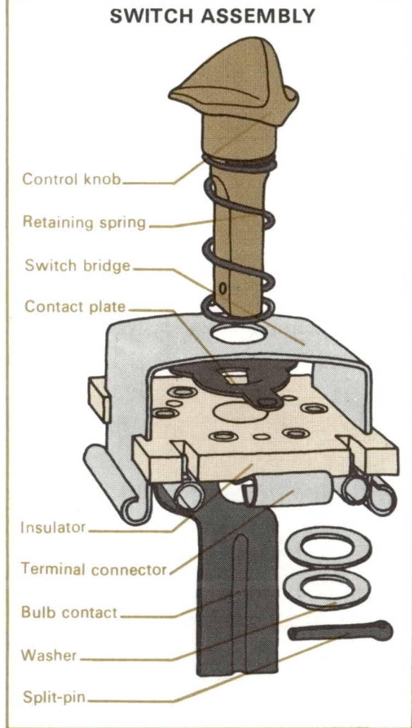

1 Clean all terminals and ensure that their shanks are fitted with plastic sleeves to prevent shorting

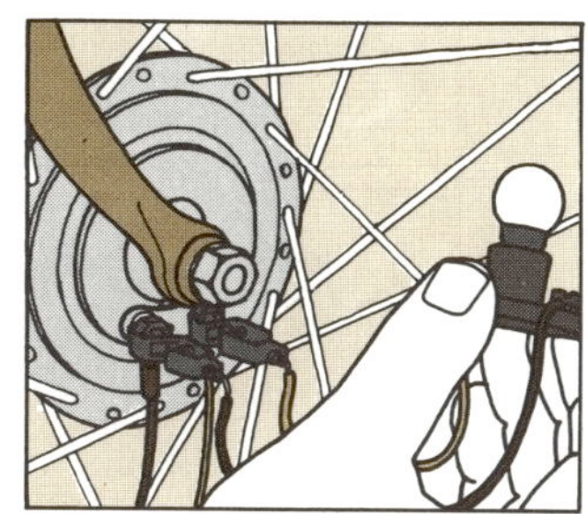

2 To test the Dynohub, connect the test leads as shown. The bulb should light when the wheel is spun

3 To test the wiring, connect the front and rear lamps in turn to the test leads and spin the wheel

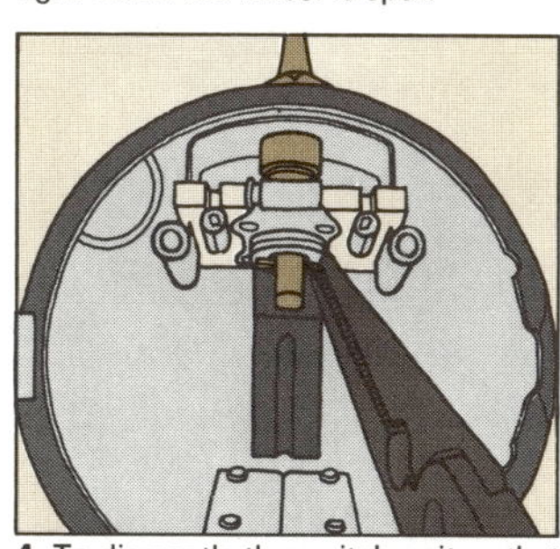

4 To dismantle the switch unit so that the switch contacts can be cleaned, withdraw the small split-pin

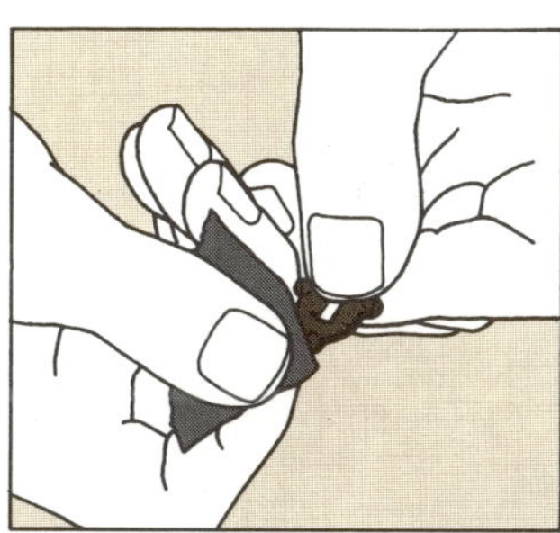

5 Lift up the switch control knob to free the three-point contact plate. Clean the plate with emery cloth

6 Lay the plate on the insulated terminal block with the pips facing downwards. Reassemble the unit

Wiring for plastic lamps

GH6 FRONT HUB AND AG REAR HUB

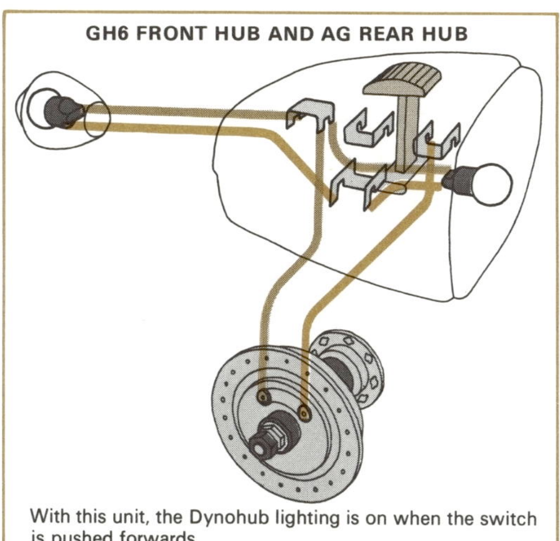

With this unit, the Dynohub lighting is on when the switch is pushed forwards

GH6 FRONT HUB WITH DRY BATTERY

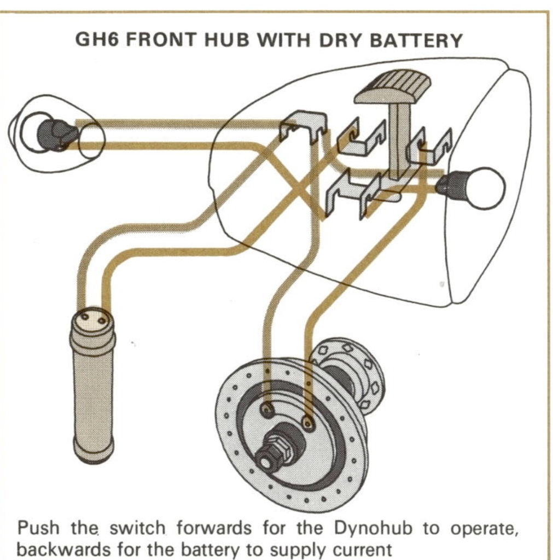

Push the switch forwards for the Dynohub to operate, backwards for the battery to supply current

Wiring

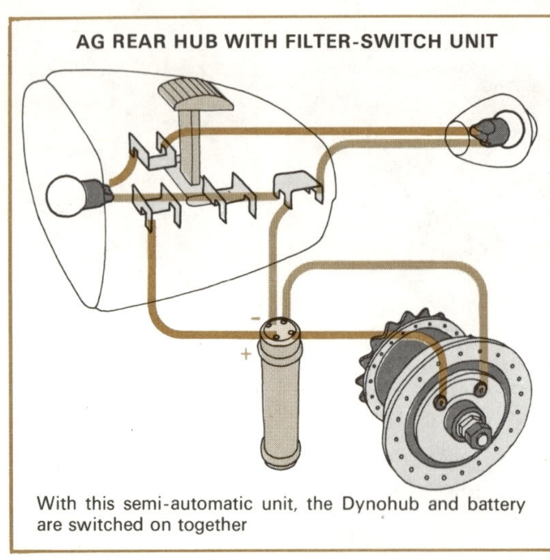

With this semi-automatic unit, the Dynohub and battery are switched on together

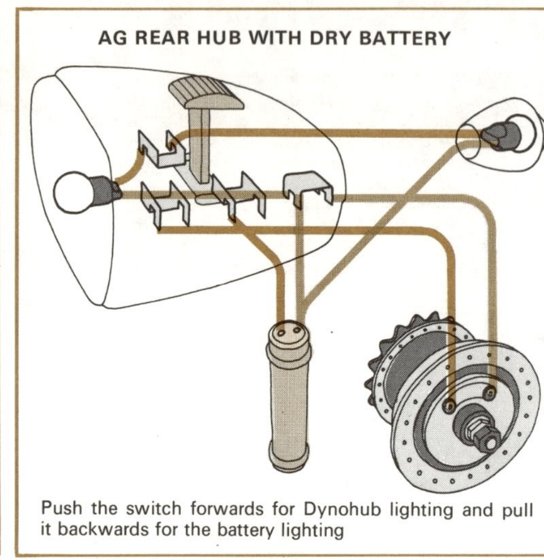

Push the switch forwards for Dynohub lighting and pull it backwards for the battery lighting

Wiring for metal lamps

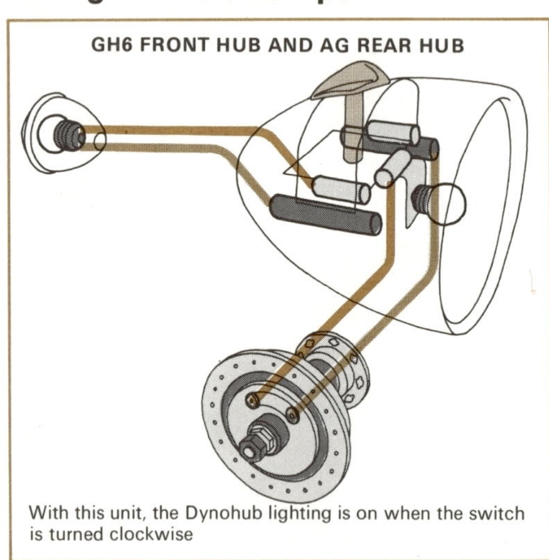

With this unit, the Dynohub lighting is on when the switch is turned clockwise

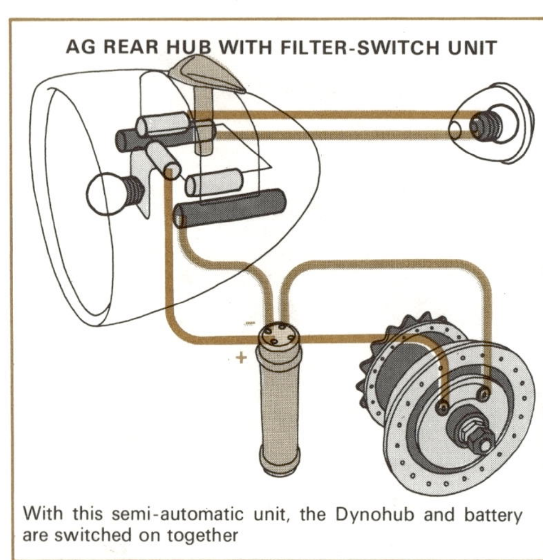

With this semi-automatic unit, the Dynohub and battery are switched on together

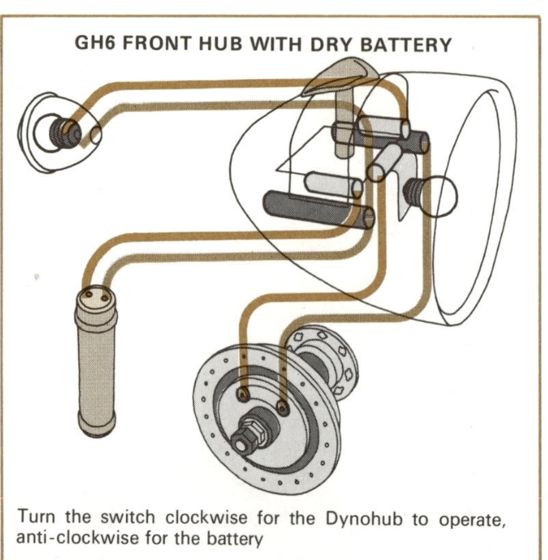

Turn the switch clockwise for the Dynohub to operate, anti-clockwise for the battery

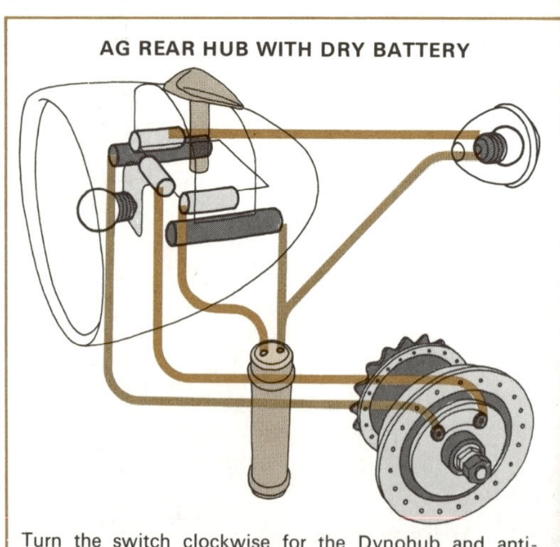

Turn the switch clockwise for the Dynohub and anti-clockwise for the battery

41-835-2